# ALCOHOL AND DRUGS:

## Research and Policy

# ALCOHOL AND DRUGS

## Research and Policy

*Edited by*
*Martin Plant, Cees Goos, Wolfram Keup and*
*Esa Österberg*

*Published on Behalf of the*
*World Health Organization, Regional*
*Office for Europe by*
*Edinburgh University Press*

© Edinburgh University Press
and World Health Organisation 1990
22 George Square, Edinburgh

Set in Lasercomp Century Schoolbook
and printed in Great Britain by
The Alden Press, London and Oxford

British Library Cataloguing
   in Publication Data
Plant, Martin A. (Martin Andrew), 1946–
Alcohol and drugs: research and policy.
1. Alcoholism & drug abuse
I. Title II. World Health Organization;
   Regional Office for Europe
362.29

ISBN 0 7486 0113 9

The views expressed in this publication are those of
the authors and do not necessarily represent the
decisions or the stated policy of the World Health
Organization.

# FOREWORD

Alcohol and drug abuse represent two of the biggest and most vexing health problems in Europe, both having their roots in the complex interplay between the individual and his/her social, cultural, economic and physical environment. While previously considered to be somewhat on the border of health concerns, alcohol and drug abuse have been brought to the forefront by the European Health for All policy and its targets.

However, they are also health problems that can be solved only through a broad approach, one that marshalls a coherent set of health-promoting, preventive and curative actions by many sectors of society working closely together. Although we already know enough to undertake broad action programmes to this end, our need for research in this is substantial, as outlined in the WHO publication *Research for Health for All* (European Health for All Series, No. 2, 1988).

The present book is about the work of scientists throughout Europe to gain further insight into alcohol and drug problems. For them, for policy makers, for anyone who has a particular interest in this area, it is not enough to know that misuse of alcohol, drugs and tobacco constitutes a major threat to the health and welfare of citizens in all European countries. To develop and implement an effective policy to deal with these problems, we need to know more. We need answers to such questions as the vulnerability of special groups, the risks associated with varying consumption levels, the kinds of changes occurring over time, and, most importantly, the effects of certain measures.

During the last two decades a substantial amount of work has been done in this area. A good basis has been laid for appropriate monitoring of trends and of effects of policy measures at national and international levels. This book gathers this work together. It is the result of one of the activities of the alcohol and drug abuse programmes of the European Regional Office of the World Health Organization. Guided by a small editorial group, the material for this book has been written by outstanding researchers and scientists. We are indebted to all who have collaborated in this activity, and particularly to the editorial group under the leadership of Dr Martin Plant.

The book shows the advances made in various parts of Europe. It also shows that regular systematic assessment processes are far from established. It is our hope that this collection will form one of the stepping stones towards this end.

J. E. ASUALL
Regional Director,
WHO Regional Office
for Europe, Copenhagen, Denmark

# CONTENTS

vii

# CONTRIBUTORS

AHLSTRÖM, S. Social Research Institute of Alcohol Studies, Helsinki, Finland.

ANOKHINA, I.P. All-Union Research Centre of Medico-biological Problems of Narcology, Moscow, USSR.

CHOQUET, M. Institut National de la Santé et de la Recherche Médicale (INSERM), Paul V. Couturier Villejuif Cedex 94807, Paris, France.

DUFFY, J. Medical Research Council Unit for Epidemiological Studies in Psychiatry, Department of Statistics, University of Edinburgh, Edinburgh, Scotland, UK.

GARRETSEN, H.F.L. Department of Epidemiology, Municipal Health Service of Rotterdam, Rotterdam, The Netherlands.

IVANETS, N.N. All-Union Research Centre on Medico-biological Problems of Narcology, Moscow, USSR.

JASINSKI, J. Institute of State and Law, Polish Academy of Science, Warsaw, Poland.

KEUP, W. Pöcking/Starnberg, Federal Republic of Germany.

KOKKEVI, A. Department of Psychiatry, Athens University Medical School, Eginition Hospital, Athens, Greece.

LEDOUX, S. Institut National de la Santé et de la Recherche Médicale (INSERM), Paul V. Couturier Villejuif Cedex 94807, Paris, France.

OLAFSDOTTIR, H. Department of Psychiatry, National University Hospital, Reykjavik, Iceland.

ÖSTERBERG, E. Social Research Institute of Alcohol Studies, Helsinki, Finland.

PLANT, M. Alcohol Research Group, Department of Psychiatry, University of Edinburgh, Edinburgh, Scotland, UK.

SIMPURA, J. Social Research Institute of Alcohol Studies, Helsinki, Finland.

STEFANIS, C. Department of Psychiatry, Athens University Medical School, Eginition Hospital, Athens, Greece.

WEISS, W. Swiss Institute for Public Health and Hospitals, Lausanne, Switzerland.

# Acknowledgements

The editors would like to thank the contributors to this book for distilling a huge amount of information and experience into short reviews. The form of this book owes much to detailed discussion of the initial draft of each chapter in Edinburgh during May 1986. All of those who attended this meeting are acknowledged for their comments and advice. This manuscript was prepared at incredible speed by Mrs Janis Nichol and Mrs Valerie Mannings of the Alcohol Research Group, University of Edinburgh. They are thanked for their efficiency and forebearance.

# Introduction

ESA ÖSTERBERG, CEES GOOS, MARTIN PLANT and
WOLFRAM KEUP

The Thirtieth World Health Assembly resolved, in May 1977, that 'the main social target of governments and the World Health Organization in the coming decades should be the attainment by all citizens of the world by the year 2000 of a level of health that will permit them to lead a socially and economically productive life' (resolution WHA 30.43). On the occasion of the Thirtieth Session of the Regional Committee at Fez in 1980 the representatives of member states of the World Health Organization (WHO) European Region approved their first common health policy: the European strategy for attaining health for all by the year 2000 (document EUR/RC30/R8 Rev.2.).

This strategy called for a fundamental change in countries' health developments and outlined four main areas of concern: lifestyles and health; risk factors affecting health and the environment; reorientation of the health-care system itself; and, finally, the political, management, technological, personnel, research and other support necessary to bring about the desired changes in these three areas. The strategy also called for the formulation of specific regional targets to support its implementation.

Altogether 38 targets in support of the European regional strategy for health for all have been specified (Targets for Health for All 1985). Alcohol and drugs are mentioned in Target 17, according to which 'by 1995, in all member states, there should be significant decreases in health-damaging behaviour, such as overuse of alcohol and pharmaceutical products; use of illicit drugs and dangerous chemical substances; and dangerous driving and violent social behaviour'. Tobacco smoking is mentioned in Target 16 where it is stated that 'by 1995, in all member states

1

there should be significant increases in positive health behaviour, such as balanced nutrition, non-smoking, appropriate physical activity and good stress management'. In *Targets for Health for All* it is furthermore specified that the attainment of Target 17 could be significantly supported by developing integrated programs aimed at reducing the consumption of alcohol and other harmful substances by at least 25 per cent by the year 2000. It is also specified that the aim of discouraging tobacco use could be achieved if clear goals were set in each member state: for example a minimum of 80 per cent of the population as non-smokers and a 50 per cent reduction in national tobacco consumption. In many countries the misuse of alcohol and prescribed or medical drugs causes far more widespread harm than does the misuse of illicit drugs such as heroin and cocaine. Even so, intravenous drug use is now an important means whereby HIV infection is being spread. This greatly increases the health risks associated with the sharing of injecting equipment by users of illicit drugs.

An informal meeting that was held at the WHO's Regional Office in Copenhagen on 30 and 31 May 1985 focussed attention on the indicators whereby progress in reducing alcohol, tobacco and drug-related harm might be assessed.

Those attending the 1985 Copenhagen Meeting concluded that, among other things, a 'consultation' was required to clarify further the special methodological problems involved in conducting surveys on alcohol and drug use, and the uses of surveys as a method of collecting data to monitor trends. During October 1985 another small working group convened in Copenhagen to arrange the proposed consultation. As a result of these activities the WHO's Regional Office for Europe and the Alcohol Research Group in the University of Edinburgh organised a Consultation on *Problems Related to Alcohol and Psychoactive Drugs*. This was held from 26 to 30 May 1986 in Edinburgh, Scotland. This book is based on material especially produced for that meeting and subsequently extensively revised.

The objectives of the Edinburgh meeting were threefold:

1) To consider methodological problems in the collection of data on the distribution within the population of the consumption of alcohol, tobacco, prescribed and illicit drugs.

2) To distinguish methodological problems in the identification of 'high consumption' groups in the population and problems involved in epidemiological studies of such groups.

2

E. ÖSTERBERG, C. GOOS, M. PLANT, and W. KEUP

3) To consider strategies to be employed in reducing consumption and adverse consequences in identified 'high risk' groups.

One of the most practical, and sometimes even the only, way to collect data on the distribution of alcohol, tobacco and drug consumption and their consumption by age and sex is to use surveys. It is widely known that surveys have many limitations. The papers presented and discussed during the Edinburgh meeting were largely related to these problems and attempted to give examples of methods which have or have not worked in practice. It was also hoped that authors could discuss the relevance of methods and solutions used, for instance, in the alcohol field, which could also be applied to the tobacco and drug fields. Furthermore, the indicators and results which may be produced by using surveys were related to practical policy perspectives by discussing prevention. As noted above, the advent of AIDS has greatly increased the health risks associated with some forms of drug use. Epidemiological studies are urgently needed to indicate the patterns and relationships between psychoactive drug use and risk of HIV infection.

Surveys have been used more widely in relation to alcohol than in relation to tobacco, prescribed and illicit drugs. This is why this book concentrates more on alcohol than on tobacco and drug surveys. Part I deals with alcohol surveys and their problems. It begins with a description by Jerzy Jasinski of alcohol, tobacco and drug surveys in Poland. The next chapter consists of a review by Jussi Simpura of the role of surveys in collecting data related to alcohol consumption. This focuses on methods and problems that are relevant in indicating the shape of the distribution of alcohol consumption and in identifying heavy drinkers. The reviews by Jasinski and Simpura are discussed by John Duffy.

The comparability and defects of survey methods are reviewed more thoroughly by Hildigunnur Ólafsdóttir. Her discussion is mainly based on alcohol survey material from Iceland and other Nordic countries. In the next chapter the system of collecting information on 'alcoholism' and alcohol problems in the USSR, and the difficulties of attaining comparability, are discussed by Irina Anokhina and Nikolai Ivanets. This contribution is discussed by Martin Plant.

The next two chapters also concentrate on alcohol and, in particular, on alcohol-related problems. The first, by Henk Garretsen, discusses the experience of using a survey as a method of collecting data on alcohol consumption and alcohol-related problems in a community study. Secondly, Salme Ahlström discusses the use of a survey to examine alcohol use and alcohol-related problems amongst adolescents. The last chapter in this section, by Esa Österberg, deals with the relationship between alcohol consumption patterns and harmful consequences. Österberg also discusses some alternative approaches to the collection of information on the relationship between drinking and alcohol-related problems.

Part II focuses upon some more specific questions. The discussion of non-survey methods is elaborated by Marie Choquet and Silvie Ledoux. Next, Anna Kokkevi and Costas Stefanis provide a practical example and describe some of the results of two Greek surveys of licit and illicit substances use and related problems. The chapter by Wolfram Keup discusses the important topic of polydrug use and misuse.

The next two chapters concentrate on prevention. In a review by Walter Weiss, and a commentary by Wolfram Keup, user careers and their implications for the prevention of misuse are discussed. Finally Martin Plant briefly reviews the complex aetiological theories which have been advanced to explain drug-related behaviour, and the implications of these theories for public policy and prevention.

# PART ONE
## SURVEYS AND THEIR
## LIMITATIONS

# 1. Methods of Data Collection from the General Population which relate to Alcohol, Tobacco and Illicit Drug Use: The Polish Experience

JERZY JASINSKI

*Abstract*. This chapter discusses alcohol, tobacco and illicit drug surveys in Poland. Some methodological problems are identified and attention is focused upon sampling. It is noted that it is difficult to ensure due representation of heavy drinkers in surveys. The impact of under-reporting is discussed, together with the merits and limitations of quota sampling in surveys of self-reported alcohol consumption.

## Introduction

The history of alcohol consumption surveys in Poland is relatively short. It began in the 1960s with two surveys conducted by A. Swiecicki. In these, as well as in subsequent surveys, national samples of population were examined. These surveys were preceded and accompanied by a number of studies of behaviour, attitudes, and opinions related to drinking amongst some special subgroups of the population, such as young people, university students, people in particular localities and workers in specific occupations.

The first survey of tobacco use, based on a national sample, was carried out in 1974. Studies of tobacco use, like those related to consumption, were preceded by studies of behaviour, attitudes, and opinions concerning smoking amongst specific groups, such as secondary school pupils, university students and doctors.

This review of different methods of data collection is largely based upon the Polish experience of alcohol and tobacco surveys. In spite of growing concern engendered by the increased use of illicit drugs such as cannabis and heroin there have been no general population surveys of the use of such substances. Even so, one survey of alcohol consumption did include a few questions on

7

the use of medical and illicit drugs (Zielinski 1986). This is referred to below.

### SURVEYS OF ALCOHOL USE

The first national survey of alcohol consumption was carried out in Poland in 1961. It was based on a sample of the population aged 20 and over. A second study was conducted in 1962 and related to people aged 18 and over.

In the first of these surveys, a short questionnaire was used, which was slightly modified for use in the second study. Apart from the introductory part concerned with food, both of these instruments contained questions on subjects such as soft drinks, type of alcoholic beverages, reasons for drinking, details of companions on the last drinking occasion and views on the acceptability of drinking by young people (Swiecicki 1963, 1964, 1968, 1986).

The third survey by Falewicz (1972) was carried out in 1968 and was based on a sample of people aged 18 and over. It examined leisure activities, relations with others within the family and at work or school. In addition data were elicited on drinking companions and location during respondents' last drinking occasion. Details were also obtained on the types and quantities of different beverages consumed, and of attitudes towards the acceptability of drinking by males and females. The latter were related to the evaluation of an alcohol education campaign.

A fourth survey by Janik (1978) related to people aged 16 and over; data were collected during 1976. Respondents were asked how often they had consumed wines, beers or spirits in the previous year, about their last drinking occasions and their general drinking patterns. Some questions also examined views on the types of people who drink more than average and on strategies to lead people to drink less.

A fifth survey, conducted in 1980, was related to a sample of people aged 16 and over (Jasinski 1984a, 1984b, 1985, Moskalewicz 1986).

The preliminary part of the questionnaire used in this study referred to the relationships of respondents with other people. Other questions were related to last drinking occasion: when it occurred, type and amounts of beverage consumed, the location of drinking, number of companions and reasons for drinking. Other questions concerned the consumption of illegal 'moonshine' alcohol, and drinking at work. The last part of the questionnaire referred to 'good' and 'bad' experiences with alcohol.

A sixth alcohol survey was conducted in 1984 by Zielinski and his colleagues (e.g. Zielinski 1986). This was the most comprehensive Polish alcohol study, and related to a sample of people aged 15 or over. This investigation examined the factors noted above, together with attitudes to permissible drinking ages for boys and girls, drinking at work, the attitudes of respondents' parents to alcohol, the use of alcohol as medication and the self-reported use of illicit drugs by respondents. Information about alcohol consumption included details of respondents' last three drinking occasions and of their first use of alcohol.

At virtually the same time as this exercise was conducted another survey was also carried out. The latter was confined to two cities, Warsaw and Krakow. Data were obtained from people aged 15 and over. This study was notable since it was designed to assess the impact of an appeal on drinking issued by the Roman Catholic Church. This had urged the Polish people to refrain from drinking spirits and to cut their consumption of wine and beer during August 1984 (Bielewicz 1985). Other appeals were issued in 1985 and 1986, and similar surveys were conducted in August 1985 (Bielewicz 1986). A more comprehensive survey was also conducted in August 1986, in order to gauge the effects of these appeals.

A seventh national sample survey was conducted by the author in 1985. To ensure comparability with earlier studies, a questionnaire was issued that was similar to that employed for the fifth survey. The main differences between these instruments were that in the 1985 survey questions were added on motives for drinking. In addition more detailed information was collected on the last occasion when wine and spirits had been consumed together with details of the duration – in hours – that these occasions lasts. The CAGE questionaire (Ewing and Rouse 1970, Ewing 1984), was also administered. This is a widely used instrument for measuring self-reported alcohol problems. Some questions, such as those concerning the consumption of spirits, were added to a routine survey of public opinion. These results are not yet available.

## SURVEYS OF DRUG AND TOBACCO USE

As noted above, the only Polish national population survey which has examined illicit drug use was mainly concerned with alcohol consumption. This was conducted in 1984, and elicited information on the respondent's use of prescribed drugs such as sedatives, tranquillisers, sleeping pills, analgesics, or stimulants (Zielinski 1986). Details were obtained of the type of drugs used, when these were last taken and how often they had been used during the last year. If prescribed by a physician, details were collected on whether the respondent had been taking them in larger quantities or more often than intended. Data were also collected about the use of illicit drugs such as cannabis and opiates. Respondents were asked which drugs they had used, when they had last taken them and how often such substances had been used during the previous year.

Only four surveys of tobacco use have been carried out in Poland: These were conducted in 1974 (Otawska 1975), in 1980 (Oles 1980), in 1982 (Zatonski 1984) and in 1985. The results of the last survey have not yet been published. Each of these studies was based on random samples and related to people aged 16 years and over.

The questionnaire used in 1974 contained only two items on respondents' smoking habits (the number of cigarettes smoked per day, and on attempts to stop smoking). In addition, a few other questions examined related issues such as smoking practices at respondents' work places, knowledge of risks connected with smoking and the existence of smoking restrictions in the country. The 1980 survey covered the same topics but in greater detail, in particular in relation to respondents' smoking habits. Other variables examined included views on the harmfulness of tobacco use, and on tobacco education. The 1982 survey concentrated on respondents' smoking habits and on the length of their exposure to nicotine. The 1985 survey also examined respondents' smoking habits, but its main focus was attitudes toward smoking and its allied health hazards.

## Sampling Problems

The first problems of surveying alcohol consumption relate to sampling. Apart from general sampling problems, the highly uneven distribution of alcohol consumption in the population has major implications. It is of great importance to ensure that 'heavy drinkers' are properly represented. Sadly it seems that whatever design is adopted such people tend to be under-represented, and those who drink most may even be missing. In the alcohol consumption surveys conducted in Poland this problem has probably had a special significance. Only one of these surveys, that of 1984, was based on a random sample of households, and even this excluded persons living in institutional accommodation, such as convents, hospitals, hostels for young people or blue-collar workers, and military barracks. It is probable that heavy drinkers are particularly numerous among the latter two categories. Other individuals excluded from such samples are those who cannot be traced or contacted, or those who refuse to co-operate. When random samples are used some estimates of the consequences of such non-response when contacted may be attempted. Such shortcomings are important and should not be ignored.

## Quota Samples

When a quota sample is used, such difficulties do not in theory occur. A quota sample does not select specific individuals or households. Instead, fieldworkers have to collect data from a sample that is defined in general terms in relation to key variables such as age, sex, race, socio-economic status or geographical location. For example, an interviewer might be required to elicit data from thirty people, half of whom are males and two-thirds of whom are manual workers. The quota approach enables non-respondents to be replaced by others sharing the required characteristics. In all Polish surveys (except for that of 1984) quota samples were used which probably exacerbated the omission of some categories of individuals. Approximately 70 per cent of the alcohol consumed in Poland is in the form of spirits, and people often drink to become intoxicated (Moskalewicz 1981). The heavy drinkers are amongst those who are rather hard to interview. They frequently cannot be contacted at home, and, if accessible, they are either sleeping or are not sober enough to be interviewed. In general they are uncooperative when asked questions about their drinking practices. Since in quota survey the final choice of respondents in any specific category rests with the interviewer, it seems highly probable that the heaviest drinkers may be avoided and excluded from the sample.

## Concealing and Forgetting

Since the systematic direct observation of drinking practices does not seem feasible as a way of measuring alcohol consumption in the general population, indirect methods are required. The most common technique is to rely on the self-reports of survey respondents. Such reports are, however, fraught with several possible distortions, the most important of which are forgetting and concealing. These distortions may be confused, since to atttribute bias to 'forgetting' may be misleading. The reason may be deliberate concealment.

No special research has been carried out in Poland on the impact of concealing and forgetting on the results of surveys of alcohol use. In general, more recent events are better remembered than those less recent, although this may not be the case in older people. It has been shown that reporting on past drinking occasions is more subject to forgetting than is informing about recent drinking (Mäkelä 1971, Knight and Wilson 1980). There is evidence of the influence of under-reporting in surveys of alcohol use (Pernanen 1974, Plant, Peck and Samuel 1985).

*Problems in Tobacco Surveys.* Distortions stemming from sampling difficulties and the forgetting or concealing of consumption are not as evident in tobacco use surveys as they are in relation to alcohol. In spite of the skewed distribution of tobacco use, heavy smokers are not as inaccessible as are heavy drinkers for survey researchers. In Poland tobacco use is widely tolerated, the anti-smoking movement being rather weak and poorly organised. Therefore, it is unlikely that the habit of smoking would be concealed from an interviewer. It has been suggested that this situation will soon change, since the anti-tobacco movement is expected to gain some momentum.

Forgetting may be less common in relation to tobacco than it is for alcohol, since most tobacco users smoke regularly, and their consumption remains fairly stable over a long period of time. However, forgetting is also an issue in tobacco use research, but takes on a different form than in alcohol consumption surveys. In examining alcohol intake, the stress is put on *current* drinking habits. This approach is exemplified by the widely accepted practice of grouping together lifelong abstainers with those who had not drunk in the year before interview. In contrast, in surveys of smoking habits much attention is paid to the duration and intensity of exposure to tobacco. This requires investigating past events which may be only poorly recalled. This is particularly likely to occur to people with irregular smoking habits.

*Estimating Alcohol Consumption.* There are two main ways of questionnaire inquiry into the drinking practices of respondents in the general population. The first of these is to ask about a specific drinking occasion (or occasions). The second is to ask each respondent to estimate his or her drinking during a specified period of time. The first approach has several possibilities: one of them is to ask about the last drinking occasion (e.g. Kuusi 1957).

All Polish surveys of alcohol use except that of 1984 have adopted this approach. Another strategy involves asking about a specific number of recent occasions, or, separately, about almost all drinking occasions which occurred over a definite period of time, usually a week (e.g. Mäkelä 1971, Dight 1976).

The second approach consists of obtaining a general estimation by the respondents of their frequencies of drinking and the amounts of alcohol consumed over a specified period. This may be 24 hours (e.g. Sadoun, Lolli and Silverman 1965); seven days (e.g. Withrich 1979); three months (e.g. Polish alcohol consumptions surveys of 1976 and 1984). Both of these approaches are often combined, in particular, to get some impression of the consistency of replies obtained.

An important advantage of the 'last occasion' approach is its simplicity, and the minimisation of forgetting because of the recency of this event for most people. This approach has a disadvantage since it relies upon one particular event. The 'last occasion' approach is sometimes used as if to suggest that the last drinking session was typical of the drinking habits of the respondent. This is a naïve assumption which should either be avoided or supported by other evidence.

Details of consumption on the last drinking occasion may suffice to group people into clear categories. More information is needed to attain accurate estimates of alcohol consumption. Such estimates should be based on fairly precise measures of individual consumption rather than on vague and general measures of what is consumed by 'light' or 'heavy' consumption.

Respondents may be grouped according to the amount of alcohol they have reportedly consumed. In this case it is assumed that every respondent was included in the subgroup to which he or she really belongs according to his or her actual drinking habits. This assumption is probably not very realistic. It is mentioned here only to emphasize that estimates based on 'last occasion' data may be inaccurate.

The approach chosen in the 1984 Polish survey, that of asking about the three last occasions, is in some way superior to the one adopted in other Polish studies. Unfortunately, it also had disadvantages. One of them is a considerable loss of information about the consumption of particular beverages: if, for example, on the last three occasions the respondent happened to drink only spirits, he or she is considered as a non-drinker of wine and beer, which may not be true. In other Polish surveys respondents were

13

separately asked about the last occasion during which they consumed spirits, wine and beer. One can argue that this is also a 'three last occasions' approach, the occasions being only chosen not according to a time sequence but according to beverage type.

For the purposes of Polish alcohol consumption surveys, total alcohol intake for each respondent was calculated on the assumption that the quantity consumed on the last occasion was typical, and that the interval between drinking occasions was twice as long as between the last occasion and the interview. Only the 1984 survey used several methods of assessing alcohol consumption. This was facilitated by the collection of information related to three consecutive drinking occasions.

### COMPARABILITY OF SURVEY RESULTS

In Poland, as in other countries, surveys of alcohol and tobacco use have been repeatedly carried out mainly to obtain information on current behaviour and to expand knowledge by examining aspects of drinking and smoking not covered by previous research. This has led to the accumulation of a large body of survey data. These constitute a valuable source of information which may be used to assess changes in drinking and smoking practices, attitudes towards alcohol and tobacco and related topics.

When planning a survey and designing an interview schedule or questionnaire a balance must be found between using old formulations, improving them or trying new approaches. A similar choice has to be made between concentrating on problems covered earlier and examining new topics. Innovation has undermined the preservation of earlier approaches in Polish survey research on alcohol and tobacco.

Apart from the well-known problems related to comparing data derived from different pieces of research, there seem to be special difficulties involved in surveying alcohol consumption and, to a lesser extent, tobacco use. These stem from sampling problems (noted above) and under-reporting by respondents. These are the main factors which cause results to be biased. There is little evidence that such bias does not change over time. Therefore, apparent changes, in particular those in drinking patterns, may be real or may result from including more heavy drinkers, or may reflect changing attitudes towards drinking which lead to more or less under-reporting. Changes in attitudes and drinking habits should first be compared in groups of people consuming similar amounts of alcohol. Accordingly, Polish survey data permit only a cautious and tentative assessment of changing trends in attitudes towards alcohol and tobacco and in the patterns of the use of these substances.

## Conclusions

The Polish experience of alcohol and tobacco surveys has some general relevance although this is constrained both in terms of time and method. Surveying alcohol consumption and tobacco use has become a routine procedure which is undertaken periodically. Quota samples have little merit except perhaps in pilot studies. It is to be hoped that future Polish surveys will be carried out on random samples of the population, like the 1984 survey and the supplementary part of that conducted in 1985.

A number of sampling problems in alcohol research remain unresolved. It is doubtful whether those who are the heaviest drinkers can be well represented in a general population sample. In order to study the size of this subgroup and their drinking habits new research is needed. This need not have a high priority, since there is a considerable literature about heavy drinkers. This is mainly based upon clinical data.

Forgetting and concealing are common problems in survey research. These do not appear to be as serious in relation to tobacco use surveys as they are in relation to alcohol use.

In surveying alcohol consumption the 'last occasion approach' has advantages for use in periodic surveys which monitor general trends in drinking habits. More ambitious projects could usefully employ detailed interviews which examine all drinking occasions over a given period of time.

REFERENCES

Bielewicz, A. (1985) *Przeglad Katolicki* 73, 30, 32–3.
Bielewicz, A. (1986) Sonataz, *Przeglad Katolicki* 74, 34.
Dight, S.E. (1976) *Scottish Drinking Habits*, London: HMSO
Ewing, J.A. (1984) Detecting alcoholism. The CAGE Questionnaire. *The Journal of the American Medical Association*, 252, 1905–7.
Ewing, J.A. and Rouse, B.A. (1970) Identifying the hidden alcoholics. Paper presented at the 29th International Congress on Alcohol and Drug Dependence, Sydney, Australia, Feb. 3.
Falewicz, J.K. (1972) *Spozycie alkoholu w Polsce i jego uwarunkowania* Warszawa, Komitet do Spraw Radia i Telewizji 'Polskie Radio i Telewizja'.
Janik, J. (1978) Wzory picia alkoholu, *Actualnosci Radiowo-Telewizyjne* 21, 16, 5–18.
Jasinski, J. (1984a) Spozycie napojow alkoholowych w Polsce w 1980 r. *Archiwum Kryminologii* 11, 7–92 (English summary, 271–8).

## Methods of data collection

Jasinski, J. (1984b) *Badania Ankietowe Nad Spzyciem Alkoholu w Polsce w 1980 roku.* Warszawa: Spoleczny Komitet Przeciwalkoholowy.

Jasinksi, J. (1985) *Spozycie Alkoholu w Opinii Publicznej,* Warszawa, Komitet do Spraw Radia i Telewizji Polskie Radio i Telewizja.

Knight, I. and Wilson, P. (1980) *Scottish Licensing Laws,* London, HMSO. Appendix C. The effect of memory on recall of alcohol consumption over the previous seven days.

Kuusi, P. (1957) *Alcohol Sales Experiment in Rural Finland,* Helsinki: The Finnish Foundation for Alcohol Studies.

Mäkelä, K. (1971) *Measuring the Consumption of Alcohol in the 1968–1969 Alcohol Consumption Study,* Helsinki: Social Research Institute of Alcohol Studies, No. 2.

Moskalewicz, J. (1981) Alcohol: Commodity and symbol in Polish society. In Single, E., Morgan, P. and de Lint, J. (eds) *Alcohol, Society and the State,* vol. 2. The Social History of Control Policy in Seven Countries, pp. 9430, Toronto: Addiction Research Foundation.

Moskalewicz, J. (1986) Obecne tendencje w zroznicowaniu spozycia w Polsce. In Wald, I. (ed) *Alkohol oraz zwiazane z nim problemy spoleczne i zdrowotne,* pp. 90–4, Warszawa: Panstwowe Wydawnictwo Naukowe.

Oles, P. (1980) Rozmiary zjawiska palenia tytoniu w Polsce. In *Problemy Higieny,* Part II, 287–304.

Otawska, E. (1975) Palic – nie palic, *Aktualnosci Radiowo-Telewizyjne* 17–18, 8, 14–19.

Pernanen, K. (1974) Validity of survey data on alcohol use. In Gibbins, R.J., Israel, Y., Kalant, H., Popham, R.E., Schmidt, W. and Smart, R.G. (eds) *Research Advances in Alcohol and Drug Problems,* vols. 1, pp. 355–374, New York: Wiley.

Plant, M.A., Peck, D.R. and Samuel, R. (1985) *Alcohol, Drugs and School-Leavers,* London: Tavistock.

Sadoun, R., Lolli, G. and Silverman, M. (1965) *Drinking in French Culture,* New Brunswick: Rutgers Centre of Alcohol Studies.

Swiecicki, A. (1963) *Struktura spozycia napojow alkoholowych w Polsce na podstawie badan ankietowych,* Warszawa, Glowny Spoleczny Komitet Przeciwalkoholowy.

Swiecicki, A. (1964) Spozycie napojow alkoholowych w Polsche w swietle badan ankietowych, *Archiwum Kryminologii* 2, 293–396 (English summary, 385–391).

Swiecicki, A. (1968) *Alkohol. Zagadnienie polityki spolecznej,* 2nd ed. (1977), Warszawa, Spoleczny Komitet Przeciwalkoholowy.

Swiecicki, A. (1986) Zroznicowanie konsumentow alkoholu. In Wald, I. (ed) *Akohol oraz zwiazane z nim problemy spolexzne i zdrowotne,* pp. 79–89, Warszawa: Panstwowe Wydawnictwo Naukowe.

Wuthrich, P. (1979) *Alkhohol in der Schwiez,* Stuttgart: Huber.

Zatonski, W. (1984) The frequency and distribution of tobacco smoking in Poland, *Przeglad Tytoniowy,* 2, 126–7.

Zielinski, A. (1986) *Social Norms Related to Alcohol.* Paper presented at the ICAA 32nd International Institute on the Prevention and Treatment of Alcoholism, Budapest, Hungary, June 1–6.

# 2. Problems in Data Collection from the General Population related to Alcohol, Tobacco and Illegal Drug Use

JUSSI SIMPURA

*Abstract.* The aims of general population studies of drugs use are different for specific substances. There is an important distinction between studies which focus on individuals and those which focus on groups or populations. General population surveys provide the best single way to obtain information on the distribution of consumption and of the prevalence of drug problems. Methods of eliciting data on consumption levels are reviewed and some key problems are identified and discussed.

## Introduction

This review discusses the methods of measuring consumption of psychoactive drugs in questionnaire studies and interview surveys. Problems related to sampling and response rates are omitted because of limitations of space. These have already been discussed in Chapter 1.

### THE GOALS OF GENERAL POPULATION SURVEYS ON SUBSTANCE USE

The main goals of general population surveys of substances use and misuse are as follows:

1. To determine the *prevalence of use and non-use* of specific substances in the population.

2. To determine the *frequency* of use among users.

3. To determine the *frequency of specific instances* of use (e.g. occasions of heavy drinking, or the use of specific types of cigarettes).

4. To obtain information on the *volume of consumption* by individuals, in subpopulations, or in the overall population.

17

5. To identify *individuals at risk* and to determine their numbers in the population.

6. To obtain information about the *relationship between the level of consumption and various consequences.*

7. To obtain information about *the shape of consumption distribution* and its possible connection to the level of aggregate consumption.

An important distinction exists between research into individual behaviour, and that related to the behaviour of groups. Traditionally, much of public health and clinical research have emphasized information on individuals, whereas sociological research pays more attention to groups. For instance, the issue of the distribution of alcohol consumption in the general population is one of the central concerns in sociological alcohol research (*see* e.g. Skog 1985, Duffy 1985), but is often omitted in the more individually-oriented research on the use of other substances.

This chapter mainly emphasizes alcohol, but tobacco, prescribed drugs and illicit drugs are also referred to. The key problems of research vary for different substances. The emphasis in research reflects different views on the aetiology of problematic use and on the means of prevention, control and treatment of problems related to excessive use.

Substance use is always a sensitive topic with the inherent problems of measurement (cf. Marquis *et al.* 1986, Stanton 1977). These topics are also discussed extensively in standard textbooks on survey methodology, such as those by Rossi *et al.* (1983) or Sudman and Bradburn (1983). Even so it may be claimed that alcohol and tobacco are less sensitive topics than either prescribed or illicit drugs. The frequency of use varies for different substances, and this is reflected in the methods of measurement. Smoking is often part of daily routine, drinking is mostly woven into the complex matrix of ordinary everyday life, but the use of prescribed and illicit drugs is generally, though not always, less commonplace. The regularity of the behaviour in question also varies. Substances which are only rarely used are more difficult to examine through survey research.

## PRACTICAL APPROACHES TO PROBLEMS OF MEASUREMENT; EXAMPLES FROM ALCOHOL RESEARCH

Although the problems of measurement vary for different substances, the main alternative approaches to data collection are probably fairly similar for all drugs.

There are a few interesting recent works on the problems of measurement of alcohol consumption in general population surveys (e.g. Room 1985 on American surveys). Mäkelä (1982), Alanko (1984) and Duffy (1985) have discussed the statistical aspects of data collection. Poikolainen and his collaborators (Poikolainen 1985a, Poikolainen and Kärkkäinen 1983, 1985) have compared various methods of data collection. Poikolainen 1985b has also discussed the role of survey work from the perspective of alcohol and health. Recent surveys of drinking practices (e.g. Enriquez de Salamanca (1984), Knibbe, Lemmens and Tan (1985), Wilson (1980), Simpura (1981), Simpura (1987)) provide useful examples and have reviewed many of the problems of measurement.

As noted by Jasinski in Chapter 1, there are basically two main alternatives to measuring consumption in general population surveys. The first is to *list* the respondent's *recent occasions* of consumption, including the amounts consumed, and the second is to let the respondents *summarize* their behaviour, e.g. in 'typical' frequencies and in 'typical' amounts per occasion. Listing occasions provides a good description of types of behaviour and fairly good consumption measures, but is not ideal for dividing drinkers into various categories. The summary method is basically oriented towards the classification of drinkers, but also provides consumption estimates. Both approaches have a number of variations. Room (1985) has noted that the 'summary approach' is typically an American tradition, whereas the method based on listing occasions is more popular in Europe. In fact, this is only partly true, since European researchers have used widely different methods. The idea of listing specific occasions has been applied in Finnish studies since the 1960s (Mäkelä 1971) and in British studies since the 1970s (Dight 1976, Wilson 1980). Examples of the summary approach in Europe are the long series of Norwegian questionnaires (Nordlund 1979), the recent Swiss studies (Muller 1983) and the Scandinavian Drinking Survey from 1979 (Simpura 1981). Also Dutch studies, described by Knibbe *et al*. (1985) seem to have applied a modification of this approach. A Spanish study (Enriquez de Salamanca 1984) provides an example of a hybrid method for calculating consumption distributions.

One of the earliest attempts to employ listing of consumption on specific occasions to generate consumption estimates was the technique of surveying one or two most recent occasions. Consumption estimates were then derived with the assumption that the distance from the most recent occasion, or the distance between the two most recent occasions, could be taken as an indicator of drinking frequency. However, these estimates can be shown to be biased (Ekholm 1972). Another classic approach is the quantity–frequency (Q–F) method (Cahalan, Cisin and Crossley 1969). This builds on the summary approach with questions on typical quantities and frequencies. One of the more recent variations is the time–line method (Sobell, Sobell and Klajner 1986). This involves respondents providing estimates of the number of days falling into mutually exclusive categories of drinking (e.g. days of abstinence, days with one to three drinks etc.)(Simpura 1981).

Another way to look at the approaches is to consider the alternative methods of data collection (Rootman and Moser 1984). These include retrospective interviews or mail questionnaires, and diaries. The diary method has seldom been used in large studies on the quantitative behaviour of general population (*see*, however, Knibbe, Lemmens and Tan 1986), although it is the standard tool in studies on the use of time, and can also provide information on drinking (Simpura 1985a). Special drinking diaries have been successfully applied in small-scale experiments and in clinical work (Poikolainen and Kärkkäinen 1983).

The main problem in measurement has certainly been under-reporting as noted in Chapter 1. High coverage is not necessarily a guarantee of a good measurement, as results can be unsatisfactory for other reasons (*see* e.g. Room 1985, Duffy 1985). In comparisons between subpopulations, one has to suppose that under-reporting is similar on all consumption levels and amongst different demographic groups. There are some studies concerning the possibility of selective under-reporting, but their implications are not clear (Cooke and Allan 1983, Poikolainen 1985a). At the population level, the two main approaches have roughly equal merit (Simpura 1981). At the individual level, however, the method of listing occasions is fraught with problems. Depending on the length of the period to be covered, a number of respondents will report zero consumption, although they may have only temporarily abstained from drinking. More generally, individual consumption estimates obtained by listing occasions are unreliable, as an individual's consumption may vary considerably within a year (Alanko 1984), whereas the typical periods covered in listing are much shorter. The summary method is also imperfect, focusing on the interpretation of expressions such as 'typically' or 'usually' in questions aimed to provide indices of alcohol consumption.

A further problem in both approaches is that indices of consumption level cannot account for the variability of drinking even within shorter periods. In particular, this is important because many alcohol-related problems are due to intoxication rather than to prolonged heavy drinking. There are various ways to overcome this flaw. In the summary approach, questions have been formulated to cover the frequency of drinking at different levels of consumption per occasion. In the listing approach information on consumption per occasion is readily available and it can be augmented with data on duration of drinking and the respondent's weight, as has been done in Finland. (Mäkelä 1971, Alanko 1984). Room (1985) gives a detailed description of various methods in the American tradition. A recent suggestion for a measure accounting for variability is provided by Greenfield (1986), who pays special attention to the prevalence of high maximum consumption per occasion.

Poikolainen and Kärkkäinen (1985) have shown that the wording of questions may greatly influence the resulting consumption estimates. For instance, the standard questions on drinking frequencies in Finnish studies have been focused on distinguishing between several classes of near-abstainers, leaving frequent drinkers with very few alternatives. A questionnaire specifically related to the characteristics of heavy drinkers produces higher consumption estimates than does the standard procedure.

There are a few technical problems that are related to the question on comparability over time and between cultures. First is the use of different units in presenting amounts. In some cultures, there are natural units such as 'a drink', whereas such entities may not exist in other cultures. Results at least should be presented in relation to some standard concepts or measures such as centilitres of pure alcohol. Another problem is the practice of presenting results calculated in daily intake. This may be appropriate in a culture in which daily drinking is commonplace, but would be completely misleading in countries with only a small number of daily drinkers. In general, some minimal requirements should be set for the presentation of results. Such requirements might be, for instance, that 'abstainers' are always those who have not consumed any alcoholic beverage within 12 months preceding data collection, that a standard scale should be

21

developed and applied on drinking frequency and the frequency of intoxication, and an estimate of weekly consumption should be provided.

## Problems of Validity and Comparability

The goals noted above may be called *descriptive*. There is another set of goals that refer to the *validity and comparability* of data. Validity relates to the problems of coverage, i.e. to what extent the actual use of consumption is covered by survey-based estimates. Reliability relates to the levels of consistency of survey data.

Validity checks for survey results are provided by various means. Biochemical methods have been developed to be used on smoking (e.g. Vogt, Selvin and Hulley 1979, Haley, Axetrad and Tilton 1983, Sexton Nowicki and Hebel 1986) and drinking (e.g. Poikolainen, Kärkkäinen and Pikkarainen 1985), and there is often a rough agreement between the two types of indicators of any individuals smoking or drinking status. Another way is to collect information from family members or other persons close to the respondent (e.g. Bauman and Koch 1983). For legal drugs prescription data are one possible source of information about drugs such as benzodiazepines (*see* Hemminki 1982). The validity of survey-based estimates of aggregate consumption may be assessed by comparing such information with sales data (e.g. Pernanen 1974). Typically, the main problem is under-reporting, although over-reporting is also sometimes evident (Stanton 1977, Simpura and Poikolainen 1983). The coverage rate, or the proportion of survey-based consumption estimates compared to sales records, varies in drinking surveys between 20 and 60 per cent (Alanko 1984, Pernanen 1974), and has been remarkably higher in surveys of smoking (*see* Warner 1978). In some countries it has been suggested that there has been a decline in the coverage by surveys of alcohol and tobacco consumption (Knibbe *et al.* 1985, Simpura 1978, Warner 1988). Few studies have considered the problems of reliability. A notable exception is the work of Sobell *et al.* (1986).

The issue of international comparability is becoming more important because of the accumulation of data from many countries. In attempts to develop worldwide policy guidelines related to substance use and misuse comparable data are needed to assist policy evaluation. Difficulties arise even when comparing countries that are homogeneous in most of the relevant respects, as the experience from the 1979 Scandinavian Drinking Survey has shown (Simpura 1981). Still, it would greatly help if some standard minimal requirements for measurement could be developed, in order to guarantee comparability. At the same time, the number of studies that allow comparisons between two or more different points in time is also increasing, and the methodological problems of measurement are a barrier to the analysis of change over time (Müller 1983, Knibbe *et al.* 1985, Simpura 1987).

## Conclusions

This brief review shows that there are many problems of measurement, and that no standards exist to define 'good quality' survey work. Such criteria are required, not only to improve the quality of surveys, but also to attain greater comparability between studies conducted in different countries at different times. One necessary step in this direction would be more extensive and systematic reviews for each substance. Examples of such reviews already exist (for alcohol, Room (1985), Rootman and Moser (1984, Midanik (1982), Pernanen (1974); for illicit drug use, e.g. Johnston (1980) and Stanton (1977)). There are also few studies that consider the measurement problems of the use of different substances in the same context (e.g. Rootman and Smart 1985). As the number of studies is rapidly increasing, and at the same time new ideas of survey methodology are emerging, updated reviews would be required at least once in a decade. So far, publications summarizing experience from surveys on substance use have been sparse. Therefore, it seems reasonable to propose that some international agency, such as the World Health Organization, should encourage attempts to review methodological issues of measuring psychoactive substance use on a more regular basis.

REFERENCES

Alanko, T. (1984) 'An overview of techniques and problems in the measurement of alcohol consumption.' In Smart, R.G. et al.: *Research Advances in Alcohol and Drug Problems*, vol. 8, New York: Plenum Press, 209–26.

Alanko, T. (1985) *Effects of Time-Variation of Drinking on the Validity of Consumption Surveys: An Empirical Investigation Using Finnish Drinking Rhythm Data.* Paper presented at the ICAA Alcohol Epidemiology Section, Rome.

Benson, G. and Holmberg, M.B. (1985) 'Validity of questionnaires in population studies on drug-use'. *Acta Psychiatrica Scandinavica*, 71, 1: 9–18.

Cahalan, D., Cisin, I. and Crossley, H. (1969) *American Drinking Practices*, Monographs of the Rutgers center of Alcohol Studies No. 6, New Brunswick.

Cooke, D.J. and Allan, J.A. (1983) 'Self-reported alcohol consumption: a
dissimulation in a Scottish urban sample'. *Journal of Studies on
Alcohol*, 44: 617–29.

Dight, S. (1976) *Scottish Drinking Habits*. London: HMSO.

Duffy, J.C. (1985) 'Questionnaire measurement of drinking behavior in
sample surveys'. *Journal of Official Statistics*, 1: 229–34.

Ekholm, A. (1972) 'Skevheten hos ett speciellt estimat av antalet
dryckesgånger.' Appendix II in Jonsson, E. and Nilsson, T.: *Samnord-
isk undersokning av vuxna mäns alkoholvanor*. Stockholm.

Enriquez de Salamanca, R. (1984) *Estudio de los habitos de Consume de
Bebidas Alcoholicas de la Boblacion Adulta Espasola Madried*,
Madrid Ministerio de Sanidad y Consumo.

Greenfield, T.K. (1986) 'Quantity per occasion and consequences of
drinking: a reconsideration and recommendation.' *The International
Journal of the Addictions*, 21: 1059–79.

Haley, N.J., Axelrad, C.M. and Tilton, K.A. (....) 'Validation of self-
reported smoking behavior: biochemical analysis of cotinine and
thiocyanate.' *American Journal of Public Health*, 73, 10, 1204–7.

Hemminki, E. (1982) 'Problems in the measurement of psychotropic drug
consumption.' *American Journal of Hospital Pharmacology* 39: 325–29.

Johnston, L.D. (1980) *Review of general population surveys of drug abuse*.
WHO Offset Publication No. 52, Geneva, World Health Organization.

Knibbe, R.A., Drop. M.J., Van Reek, J. and Saenger, G. (1985) 'The
development of alcohol consumption in the Netherlands: 1958–1981'.
*British Journal of Addiction* 80: 411–19.

Knibbe, R.A., Lemmens, P. and Tan, F. (1986) *Weekly Recall and Diary
Estimates of Alcohol Consumption in a General Population Survey*.
Paper presented at the ICAA Alcohol Epidemiology section meeting,
Dubrovnik, June.

Marquis, K.H., Marquis, S. and Polich, J.M. (1986). 'The validity of self-
reported alcohol consumption and alcohol problems: a literature
review.' *British Journal of Addiction* 77: 357–82.

Muller, R. (1983) *Trinksitten im Wandel*. Lausanne; SFA arbeitsberichte
der forschungsabtailung Nr 13.

Mäkelä, K. (1971) *Measuring the consumption of alcohol in the 1968–69
Alcohol consumption study*. Social Research Institute of Alcohol
Studies, Helsinki.

Mäkelä, K. (1982) 'Measurement of alcohol consumption'. Manuscript,
prepared for publication in Polish in *Alcohol and Alcohol Problems*,
ed. I. Wald.

Nordlund, S. (1981) *Alkoholdata 1979*. Also: SIFA-mimeograph No. 50.

Pernanen, K. (1974) 'Validity of survey data on alcohol use'. In: Gibbins,
R.J. et al: *Research Advances in Alcohol and Drug Problems*, vol 1,
New York; Wiley, 355–74.

Poikolainen, K. (1985a) 'Underestimation of recalled alcohol intake in
relation to actual consumption.' *British Journal of Addiction* 80:
215–16.

Poikolainen, K. (1985b) *Alcohol and Health: New Perspectives for Survey
Research*. 'Paper presented at World Psychiatric Association
Symposium. 'The Future of Psychiatric Epidemiology', Edinburgh,
September.

Poikolainen, K. and Kärkkäinen, P. (1985) 'Nature of questionnaire
options affects estimates of alcohol intake'. *Journal of Studies on
Alcohol* 46: 219–22.

Poikolainen, K. and Kärkkäinen, P. (1983) 'Diary gives more accurate
information about alcohol consumption than questionnaire'. *Drug*

*and Alcohol Dependence*, 11: 209–16.

Poikolainen, K., Kärkkäinen, P. and Pikkarainen, J. (1985) 'Correlations between biological markers and alcohol intake as measured by diary and questionnaire in men'. *Journal of Studies on Alcohol* 46, 5: 383–7.

Room, R. (1985) *Measuring Alcohol Consumption in the U.S.: Methods and Rationales*. Paper presented at the ICAA Alcohol Epidemiology Section, Rome.

Rootman, I. and Moser, J. (1984) *Guidelines for Investigating Alcohol Problems and Developing Appropriate Responses*. WHO Offset Publication No. 81, Geneva, World Health Organization.

Rootman, I. and Smart, Reginald G. 'A comparison of alcohol, tobacco and drug use as determined from household and school surveys'. *Drug and Alcohol Dependence* 16, 89–94.

Rossi, P.H., Wright, J.D. and Anderson, A.B. (1983) *Handbook of Survey Research*, Academic Press, Orlando.

Sexton, M., Nowicki, P. and Hebel, J.R. (1986) 'Verification of smoking status by thiocyanate in unrefrigerated, mailed saliva samples'. *Preventive Medicine* 15, 28–34.

Simpura, J. (1981) *Construction of Indices of Alcohol Intake*. Oslo; SIFA-mimeograph 46.

Simpura, J. (1985) 'Drinking: an ignored leisure activity'. *Journal of Leisure Research* 17: 200–11.

Simpura, J. (1987) *Finnish Drinking Habits. Results from interview surveys in 1968, 1976 and 1984*. Helsinki; Finnish Foundation of Alcohol Studies.

Simpura, J. and Poikolainen, K. (1983) 'Accuracy of retrospective measurement of individual alcohol consumption in men: a reinterview after 18 years'. *Journal of Studies on Alcohol* 44: 911–17.

Skog, Ole-Jørgen (1985) 'The collectivity of drinking cultures: a theory of the distribution of alcohol consumption'. *British Journal of Addiction* 80: 83–99.

Sobell, M.B., Sobell, L.C. and Klajnar, R. (1986) 'The reliability of a timeline method for assessing normal drinker college student's recent drinking history: Utility for alcohol research'. *Addictive Behaviours* 11: 149–61.

Stanton, M.D. (1977) 'Drug use surveys: methods and madness'. *International Journal of Addiction*, 12: 95–120.

Sudman, S. and Bradburn, N.M. (1983) *Asking Questions. A Practical Guide to Questionnaire Design*. Jossey-Bass, San Francisco.

Warner, K.E. (1978) 'Possible increases in the underreporting of cigarette consumption'. *Journal of the American Statistical Associates* 73: 314–18.

Wilson, P. (1980) *Drinking in England and Wales*. HMSO, London.

Vogt, T.M., Selvin, S. and Hulley, S.B. (1979) 'Comparison of Biochemical and questionnaire estimates of tobacco exposure'. *Preventative Medicine* 8, 23–33.

# 3. Data Collection: A Methodological Response

JOHN DUFFY

The bulk of Dr Simpura's chapter relates to alcohol consumption measurement in population surveys, and this is discussed below in conjunction with his remarks on surveys of smoking and drug use.

In his list of primary goals it is useful to distinguish those aimed at (a) Group or population level description, and (b) Individual level description.

Mäkelä (1982) discussing individual measures, concluded that questions on customary habits are more reliable than eliciting actual consumption on specified occasions. However, it is necessary to distinguish between measuring consumption in order to obtain estimates of totals or means, whether for individuals or populations, and attempts to classify respondents into categories such as 'light-frequent', 'moderate occasional', etc. Mäkelä's remark could usefully be interpreted in terms of the classification of individuals rather than the estimation of total consumption.

Survey methods could hardly be expected to capture completely the potential variability in the within-individual pattern of drinking, and for most purposes such temporal variation is ignored. Simpura's comment that 'last week's consumption' methods may lead to reliable estimates of the population distribution into consumption categories should be understood as relating to the population proportions in such categories rather than to the proportion of correct *individual* classifications. In other words, a survey may indicate that, in a certain population, ten per cent of individuals consume more than 25 glasses of wine or spirits (or the equivalent amount of alcohol in beer or lager) per week. While 'ten per cent' may be a fairly accurate statement of the position, it is nevertheless emphasized that individual drinking habits vary from time to time, so it is not to be inferred

26

that specific people necessarily always drink as they did at the time of a specific survey. There is little evidence relating population distributions of consumption over long periods to sample distributions typically based on much shorter time periods. There are in a sense two dimensions to the sampling exercise – the individual and the temporal.

The secondary goals identified by Simpura relate to comparability across time within populations and comparisons between different populations. The question of which beverages to include is a greater problem for the second type of comparison.

Simpura outlines two methods of measuring consumption – the 'occasions' and 'summarial' approaches – and these are certainly the most frequently encountered methods in European and North American research in this field.

The survey by Edwards, Chandler and Hensman (1972) could be added to the list of European studies using the summarial approach. In fact this study used both summarial quantity–frequency (Q–F) and last seven days occasions measures. A secondary analysis of Edwards' data indicated that converting the summarial measures to consumption rates yielded a high correlation with consumption over the last seven days. However the latter measure yielded a higher population mean value. Needless to say, there is a lot more work to be done in the area of comparisons of measurement methods, and more sophisticated analyses could be performed.

Tobacco research is discussed below, but it is noted in passing that if there is little within-individual temporal variation in smoking behaviour then typical behaviour will be similar to actual or recent behaviour.

So far as the instruments of data collection are concerned, the use of diaries in alcohol research on general populations could be questioned. Although Poikolainen and Karkkainen (1983) showed that higher consumption levels were reported using a diary, it is generally found that such methods generate high refusal rates and that making respondents aware of their behaviour by self-monitoring may precipitate a temporary change in habits. So too may the financial inducement offered to respondents. It is notable that the subjects in the Poikolainen and Karkkainen study were volunteers obtained by advertisement, and that of the 60 so recruited, 6 withdrew from the study.

Poikolainen and Karkkainen (1985) later showed that providing very high preset categories of quantity in the summarial approach increased reported consumption. Sudman and Bradburn (1982) suggest that, even with a summarial approach, it may be better to leave responses completely open than to use categories at all. Rather than having preset categories of, for example, 1–2, 3–4, 5–7, 8–12 drinks, the respondent simply reports the actual number of drinks. A similar approach may be used for frequency questions.

Simpura's remarks concerning the shape of the consumption distribution are laudable; even so, the precise nature of the distribution is unlikely to be constant and fully determinable. As Simpura suggests, an exhaustive review is vital to international comparability, and there is great merit in modelling inter- and intra-individual variation in drinking behaviour as a series of events occurring in time with associated occasion intake.

As indicated by Duffy and Waterton (1984, 1988) alternative methods of data collection are worth considering. Definite gains may be achieved by implementing alternative techniques to the standard interview.

Dr Jasinski correctly outlines the deficiencies of quota sampling in this area. It is now generally recognised that the most suitable procedure is probability sampling. It may be necessary to supplement a sample based on a register of electors, for example, with special techniques for sampling individuals in institutional or temporary accommodation. It is also important to ensure adequate interviewer call-backs to contact as many respondents as possible.

That the problem of forgetting increases as the occasions recalled recede in time is certainly correct, but attention should be drawn to the possibility of over-estimating forgetting by analysing occasion consumption as a function of recency. Since most 'occasions' approaches ask questions in reverse temporal order, social desirability may act to increase concealment error as the interview progresses.

The remarks concerning the length and intensity of exposure to tobacco are of interest. The comparison of this topic and alcohol and tobacco surveys is noted below.

On the question of estimating total consumption Jasinski's remarks about the misclassification of individuals are well-founded. However, from the point of view of estimating a population total or mean this need not be a problem. If errors are random then the real difficulty relates to calculating an annual intake for an individual on the basis of the last occasion.

JOHN DUFFY

## General Remarks

In connection with Dr Jasinski's point about lifetime tobacco use it might be relevant to point out that a similar approach may be possible in the alcohol field. While the populations of certain countries show remarkable regularity in their alcohol consumption patterns, this is not generally the case. For non-wine-producing countries a more episodic consumption pattern is encountered. Dunham (1983) suggests that lifetime pattern of consumption and hence 'exposure' might be investigated by a pseudo-panel technique. It is too early for a considered assessment of the value of this approach, but it is worthy of further investigation by means of comparative experiments in sample surveys, particularly to assess its power as a predictor or correlate of alcohol-related problems.

On the question of comparing techniques of data collection a few points could be noted. Firstly, experience with computer interviewing, using a computerised self-administered questionnaire (CSAQ), had shown that larger quantities were reported using this method than using direct interviewing on a matched sample (Waterton and Duffy, 1984). Further, values reported in direct interviewing yielded consumption estimates consistent with previous surveys in the same geographical area. Interestingly, Sudman and Bradburn (1982) suggest the use of long questions which give subjects more time to think, and Waterton and Duffy found that CSAQ took an average of 13 minutes longer than direct interviewing.

Another method variant in sample surveys is the randomised response technique (RR). Duffy and Waterton (1984) developed such a technique for measures of last seven days' consumption which required individuals to calculate their total intake over the period, and then modify it by the addition of a randomly generated number. This study showed that, in the field, subjects had difficulty in converting their drinking into standard units. Respondents became confused when faced with extensive conversion tables.

The more familiar RR technique for qualitative responses has been used on a population sample by Duffy and Waterton (1988) to estimate alcohol problem prevalence, with rather disappointing results.

In tobacco surveys saliva thiocyanate determination may be used to validate respondents' self-reported smoking. Gillies, Wilcox, Coates, Kristmundsdottir and Reid (1982) replicated the

29

findings of Luepker, Pechacek, Murray, Johnson, Hurd and Jacobs (1980) that prior knowledge that this test would be performed increased self-reported smoking among schoolchildren. Thus proxy measures may assist in reducing the problem of concealment by increasing respondent truthfulness. In an Edinburgh alcohol survey blood samples were taken to assess the relationship between various constituents and characteristics of the blood and self-reported consumption (Chick, Kreitman and Plant 1981). It could be conjectured that the respondent's prior knowledge that such a sample would be taken might reduce deliberate concealment of consumption.

There are other interesting analogies and differences between surveys of drinking and smoking behaviour. For example, although it is generally held that smoking as a habitual behaviour shows more within-individual regularity than drinking, there may be disagreement about the related exposure, due to between-individual variation in methods of smoking. It has been suggested that variables like puff-volume, inter-puff interval and type of material smoked, vary between individuals at the same level of consumption, with resultant variation in exposure to the harmful agents in tobacco smoke (Grabowski and Bell, 1983). This problem does not normally arise, or at any rate is not often considered, in connection with alcohol surveys, in which the actual alcohol content of the beverage is considered the unitary measure.

In the field of surveys of illegal drug use there appears to have been little research into related methodological aspects. There are a few points which can be made however.

The RR technique has been used to estimate the prevalence of cannabis (use in an Australian household survey (Brewer, 1981). A subset of respondents in the 15–39 age group were questioned directly about cannabis use, the remainder in the age group being asked by an RR method. Paradoxically, the RR method produced lower prevalence estimates than direct questioning. These included proportions for 'ever used', 'used in the last four weeks' and 'used in last week'.

That drug surveys suffer from problems similar to those in the alcohol field can be seen from the finding that in one study respondents reported 2.4 to 2.9 times as many occasions of illicit drug use in the past month than would be expected from their estimates of their annual frequency of use (Bachman and O'Malley 1981). This effect was consistent across different drugs and based on large and nationally representative US samples. In general it seems

30

that under-reporting of such events increases relatively rapidly with elapsed time since the event.

Finally, it is gratifying to see so much attention now being devoted to survey research in the substance abuse area. In addition to the actual conduct of field surveys it is hoped that there will also be increased methodological research, and planned experiments to compare alternate measurement strategies. There are many colleagues wishing to improve survey methods in this field, and at the moment the methodological infrastructure is still in the process of development. Research in survey methodology holds great promise for the future.

REFERENCES

Bachman, J.G. and O'Malley, P.M. (1981) When four months equal a year: inconsistencies in student reports of drug use, *Public Opinion Quarterly* 45, 536–48.

Brewer, K.R.W. (1981) Estimating marijuana usage using randomised response – some paradoxical findings, *Australian Journal of Statistics* 23, 139–48.

Chick, J., Kreitman, N. and Plant, M.A. (1981) Mean cell volume and gamma glutamyl – transpeptidase as markers of drinking in working men, *Lancet* i, 1249–51.

Duffy, J.C. and Waterton, J.J. (1984) Randomised response models for estimating the distribution function of a quantitative character, *International Statistical Review* 52, 165–71.

Duffy, J.C. and Waterton, J.J. (1988) Randomised response vs. direct questioning: estimating the prevalence of alcohol related problems in a field survey, *Australian Journal of Statistics* 30, 1–14.

Dunham, R.G. (1983) Rethinking the measurement of drinking patterns, *Journal of Studies on Alcohol* 44, 485–93.

Edwards, G., Chandler, J. and Hensman, C. (1972) Drinking in a London suburb, *Quarterly Journal of Studies in Alcohol*, Suppl. 6, 69–128.

Gillies, P.A., Wilcox, B., Coates, C., Kristmundsdottir, F. and Reid, D. (1982) Use of objective measurement in the validation of self-reported smoking in children aged 10 and 11 years: saliva thiocyanate, *Journal of Epidemilogy and Community Health* 36, 205–8.

Grabowski, J. and Bell, C. (1983) *Measurement in the Analysis and Treatment of Smoking Behaviour*, Washington: USGPO, NIDA Research Monograph 48.

Jasinski, J. (1985) *Measurement of Drinking in Polish Alcohol Consumption Surveys*. Paper presented to Alcohol Epidemiology Section, ICAA, Rome.

Luepker, R., Pechacek, T., Murray, D., Johnson, C., Hurd, P. and Jacobs, D. (1980) *Saliva Thiocyanate: A Chemical Indication of Cigarette Smoking in Adolescents*, Minnesota: Laboratory of Physiological Hygiene, School of Public Health.

Mäkelä, K. (1982) Measurement of alcohol consumption. Prepared for Wald (ed) *Alcohol and Alcohol Problems*, Panstwowe Wydawnictwo Naukowe.

Poikolainen, K. and Karkkainen, P. (1983) Diary gives more accurate information about alcohol consumption than questionnaire, *Drug and Alcohol Dependence* 11, 209–16.

Poikolainen, K. and Karkkainen, P. (1985) Nature of questionnaire options affects estimates of alcohol intake, *Journal of Studies on Alcohol* 46, 219–22.

Sudman, S. and Bradburn, N.M. (1982) *Asking Questions*, San Francisco: Jossey-Bass.

Waterton, J.J. and Duffy, J.C. (1984) A comparison of computer interviewing techniques and traditional methods in the collection of self-report alcohol consumption data in a field survey, *International Statistical Review* 52, 173–82.

# 4. Achieving Comparability between Surveys in Different Settings

HILDIGUNNUR ÓLAFSDÓTTIR

*Abstract.* Several surveys of the use of alcohol and illegal drugs in Iceland have been carried out during the past fifteen years. Studies of the adult population have mainly been concerned with the use of alcohol, while those carried out among adolescents have also included questions on illegal drugs. Regular surveys on drinking patterns among the adult population have focused on intra-societal comparability. Some methodological problems associated with longitudinal studies are briefly discussed. The experience derived from the Scandinavian Drinking Survey is considered. Surveys on adolescent drug use have usually been carried out as single projects, and their limited comparability is discussed. Steps are proposed to increase the comparability of future surveys.

## Introduction

The changing picture of drug use in the Western world in the last few decades has increased interest in the comparison of survey results. Epidemiological surveys have been used as instruments to obtain a continuous picture of the changing patterns of the use of licit and illicit drugs in many countries. Most surveys in the alcohol and drug field have been single cross-sectional exercises, although investigators have sometimes related their results to previous research. The general level of comparability between studies has been rather low. Some countries have succeeded in organising research projects, which are carried out at regular intervals and can be compared. Trend studies of both alcohol and cannabis use among young people have been carried out, for example, in Australia, Canada, Norway and the United States of America (Smart and Murray 1981). Cross-national surveys on the use of licit and illicit drugs have not been widely developed. Comparisons have been largely restricted to literature reviews.

Comparative studies are needed to increase the understanding of alcohol and drug problems in different settings. When considering ways of improving surveys of licit or illicit drug use, it is helpful to know how previous studies have handled the problem of comparability. This chapter is, however, only concerned with the experience of previous surveys on the use of alcohol and illegal drugs in a small, modern industrialized country – Iceland. Research in the alcohol- and drug-related fields did not develop until the 1960s. Since that time such activity has gradually been increasing.

SURVEYS OF THE USE OF ALCOHOL AMONG THE ADULT
POPULATION

## Longitudinal Studies

Surveys of the use of alcohol and tobacco, as well as studies of prescribed drugs, have varied in scope and methods. However, they have produced information that indicates a general pattern of use of licit and illicit drugs in the community.

The most comprehensive surveys conducted so far have been concerned with the use of alcohol by adults. These studies were carried out in collaboration between the Department of Psychiatry at the National University Hospital in Reykjavik and the State Liquor Preventive Council. The first of these projects was a longitudinal study on the use and abuse of alcohol. This began in 1972–74, and the original sample has been examined three times at approximately five-year intervals. The most recent survey was carried out in 1984 (Helgason 1985). The purpose of this exercise was to investigate changes in the use and abuse of alcohol with the respondents' increasing age. In the most recent survey, a new sub-sample, comprising of younger individuals, was added to the original sample. This permits a two-sided comparison. It was possible to compare young people's drinking in the mid 1980s with the alcohol consumption reported by people of the same age in the beginning of the 1970s. In addition, the young respondents may also be compared with older people.

Administering longitudinal surveys is no easy task. At the outset this survey was a pioneering enterprise. In the beginning the sample was drawn only from Reykjavik, but the study developed two years later into a national survey. It must be pointed out that few surveys of any kind had been conducted in Iceland at that time. The original survey, as noted above, has since been repeated twice, with the original questionnaire only slightly altered. Some additional items have been added to this instrument to meet new interests.

Information on respondents' backgrounds has caused practical problems. While the study has been in effect, the country's educational system has undergone major changes, making comparison of the data about education difficult to achieve.

The retention of the original sample has been problematic. Icelandic people often move home. Despite the relatively high level of accuracy of official personal registers it has been difficult to trace some respondents. This has reduced response rates and is discussed below in connection with general methodological problems.

## Scandinavian Drinking Survey

Iceland participated in the Scandinavian Drinking Survey in 1979. This study was the first, and so far the only, cross-national comparative alcohol survey that Iceland has been involved with. This venture is a good example of international collaboration. The initiative for this research project came from the Nordic Board for Alcohol Research. The National Institute for Alcohol Research in Norway and the Social Research Institute of Alcohol Studies in Finland agreed to assume responsibility for the study. Researchers from these institutions, along with others from the Departments of Sociology in Linköping and Stockholm in Sweden, and from The Department of Psychiatry at the National University Hospital in Iceland, formed the research team.

The study was designed to examine drinking habits and their consequences and attitudes towards drinking among the adult populations of the participating countries. The aim was to compare the interactions between drinking behaviour, attitudes towards drinking and consequences of drinking in different cultural and structural settings.

The Nordic countries, Denmark, Finland, Iceland, Norway and Sweden, may superficially appear to be culturally fairly homogeneous. Despite this, a number of practical and theoretical problems were evident throughout the project. Some of these difficulties are revealed in the following description by two of the researchers involved in this venture (Hauge and Irgens-Jensen 1981a):

Finland, Norway and Sweden have long-standing traditions in epidemiological alcohol research by means of surveys – traditions which, unfortunately, differ from country to country. At the outset, all countries involved wanted the questionnaire to be framed in a manner which would make the resultant data comparable with those of earlier national studies. Different attitudes to alcohol and alcohol policy in the various countries also caused problems. Since financial support for the study had to come from the national sources, the questions had to be so formulated as to ensure that the financing authorities would support the study. Special consideration had to be given to Denmark, which has a more liberal attitude to alcohol than the other Scandinavian countries and which tends to be less than enthusiastic about this kind of alcohol research.

It had been planned to include Denmark in this study, but funding to facilitate this did not materialize, and Denmark did not participate.

From the outset, it was planned to gather information through identical questionnaires in each country. These were sent by mail and answered anonymously. It was decided to draw a sample of approximately 3000 subjects from each country. These comprised nationally representative samples of both sexes between the ages of 20 and 69. These samples represent different proportions of the population in the age groups concerned, because of the difference in the sizes of the populations of the four countries. Since the Icelandic population is much smaller than those of the other countries, the Iceland sample was perhaps unnecessarily large. It is convenient when subcategories are analysed, if all samples are of the same size, although this was not methodologically necessary.

Sampling, data collection, and the coding procedures were administered separately in each country. Even so, efforts were made to ensure uniform sampling and data collection procedures. However, some cultural differences made it necessary to adapt sampling methods appropriate to local conditions. Procedures were the same in Finland, Iceland and Sweden, where the samples were drawn from a universe consisting of all persons in the respective age groups from a central population register. In Norway the sampling was done in two stages. First, a subsample consisting of all persons born on certain specific dates was chosen from the universe and from this the final sample was randomly drawn. The samples in Finland, Norway and Sweden were selected from the national registers that were up to date on 31 October 1978. The Icelandic sample was drawn from a register which was updated approximately one year earlier.

In Iceland, however, a minor complication arose, because a second study of drinking habits and alcohol abuse was also being conducted. The two exercises included some of the same individuals. These people, 91 in all, were excluded from the sample drawn for the Scandinavian Drinking Survey.

There were differences between the four countries in relation to the definition of what constitutes a person's residence. There were also differences regarding people without a permanent residence, students, and people working abroad for limited periods of time. These differences between the countries may have affected response rates.

A standard procedure was followed in relation to data collection. In February 1979 questionnaires were mailed to the prospective respondents in each of the four countries, followed later by two letters of reminder. The layouts of the questionnaires and letters were the same in all four countries.

Response was lowest in Norway (54.5 per cent), somewhat higher in Sweden (58.3 per cent) and 63.1 per cent in Iceland, but was 71.3 per cent in Finland. In earlier surveys, the response rate had also been highest in Finland. The second reminder asked non-respondents to give reasons for not participating in the survey. The number of letters received with such reasons varied from 137 in Finland to 270 in Sweden. The most common reason given was that the non-respondents were opposed to answering such questionnaires. The majority of the non-respondents did not give any reason for not participating in the survey. Despite national variations in response rates, analysis of the representativeness of the samples showed that they were adequate for inter-cultural comparison.

The questionnaire included 91 items. In Iceland five additional items were included and in Sweden extra questions were added. These new questions related to topics of national interest.

The first eleven questions were concerned with demographic variables, such as age, sex, marital status, place and type of residence, length of education, current employment, occupation and income. Educational systems, occupational classifications and income levels differed from one country to another. Because of this, classification of these variables was difficult. A definition of education was made by simply asking each respondent how many years he or she had attended school or had studied. The problem of the income variable was resolved by dividing reported income into three equal segments in each country. It was not considered feasible to define the occupational classifications for uniform comparison between countries. Accordingly, this variable was only used on a national basis. The same procedure was adopted in relation to place of residence, because the residential structures in the four countries were different.

The next section of the questionnaire consisted of fourteen items on frequency and quantity of drinking and experience of intoxication.

Respondents were asked whether, in the last twelve months prior to the survey, they had consumed beer, wine or spirits, and the amount of each type they had imbibed. Despite the fact that beer stronger than 2.25 per cent alcohol of volume is prohibited in Iceland, it was decided to include identical questions on beer in the Icelandic questionnaire to those in the other three countries. This way it would be possible to cover the consumption of home-made beer, and legally and even illegally imported beer.

It was decided to employ a joint measure for reporting alcohol consumption, namely, the annual consumption of 100 per cent alcohol. The formula for the index of annual alcohol consumption included the quantity and frequency of consumption of specific beverage types. The average content of each beverage type and sizes of glasses, drinks and bottles vary in the four countries. In order to obtain comparable estimates of quantities, it was necessary to have slightly different formulas for each country.

The most exact method of calculating alcohol consumption would have been to use the average estimated alcohol content separately for each country and for each beverage type. This would have led to only minor differences in the amount of alcohol corresponding to any given alternative in each country. Individually precise measures for each respondent could not be calculated, since the range of variation of alcohol content within each beverage type was considerable in all countries. The researchers therefore estimated the range of variation for each alternative on the basis of which a rough common Nordic average was chosen. This was then applied in all countries.

The alcohol content of beer was defined as 4.5 per cent of volume, and as 14.5 per cent for wines, due to the inclusion of both natural and fortified wines. The figure decided upon for spirits was 40 per cent.

The question of how often respondents considered themselves to have been intoxicated was based upon the self-reported frequency of intoxication. Linguistic nuances may have caused differences in the patterns of answers.

The thirty-seven questions concerning attitudes towards drinking and drunkenness did not involve any particular conceptual problems. The twenty-nine questions on personal experiences related to drinking reflected subjective consequences and were not objective measures. They may have reflected cultural conditions.

National differences in alcohol research became obvious at the point of data analysis. Accordingly, it was decided to publish the results in the mimeograph series published by the National Institute for Alcohol Research in Norway, and in scientific journals rather than in one final report. So far approximately fifteen publications have appeared in this series (Hauge and Irgens-Jensen 1981a, 1981b, 1984a, 1984b, Mäkelä 1981, 1982, 1984, Simpura 1981, 1985a, 1985b, 1985c, 1985d) or as journal or anthology articles (Hauge and Irgens-Jensen 1986, Jarvinen and Olafsdottir 1984, 1986).

The Scandinavian Drinking Survey has shown that comparative research projects must be designed in the awareness of national research traditions and the practical problems encountered in different cultures, even when closely related nations are involved.

## Other Surveys

In recent years some questions concerning alcohol use or attitudes towards alcohol have been included in the Gallup Omnibus Survey which has been carried out periodically. These questions are sometimes contained in survey instruments used in different countries, but the results are seldom compared in a systematic way. Other surveys concerned with alcohol have not been carried out among the general adult population. A few studies among subgroups such as prison inmates are methodologically incomplete and are not referred to in this chapter.

Surveys of the use of tobacco have been conducted by the Icelandic Heart Association and other health organizations, but these are not cited in this review. Studies of the use of prescribed drugs have been undertaken at different intervals. These have relied on information from medical prescriptions, and, in fact, indicate prescription practice rather than the use of drugs by their recipients.

One survey conducted on licit and illicit drugs can be referred to here, because it was comprised of a sample of individuals from 16 to 36 years of age. It will be discussed in the next section because of its main emphasis on illicit drug use.

### SURVEYS OF THE USE OF DRUGS AMONG ADOLESCENTS

Surveys of the use of drugs among adolescents have been conducted for just as long as surveys among the adult population. They have been concerned with alcohol as well as illegal drugs. The first surveys of this type were conducted by separate researchers, who carried out their projects independently, sometimes with official support. These studies were conducted by young and often inexperienced investigators, who sometimes carried out drug research as part of their professional education. The samples were small, and often drawn only from the municipality of Reykjavik. Despite the fact that these surveys have been carried out as single projects, it is possible to compare data from 1972, 1980 and 1984.

Two of the most recent youth surveys, which were carried out in 1984, were national in scope. One of these was conducted on behalf of the General Director of Public Health, and the other with financial support from the Scandinavian Research Council for Criminology.

When constructing the questionnaires used in some of these surveys the investigators had taken advantage of experiences from surveys carried out in other countries. Surveys conducted by the National Institute for Alcohol Research in Norway, and by the Board of Education in Sweden, have been important models in this connection. This could have been an opportunity to compare results between national studies, but these opportunities to conduct a comparison have unfortunately been used only to a limited extent. The main emphasis has been on the national analysis, and results were not systematically compared with those from other Scandinavian surveys. However, there are a few exceptions to this (Ragnarsdottir Briem 1981, Kristmundsson 1985).

## Methodological Problems

The questionnaire has been the most popular instrument in Icelandic alcohol and drug surveys. Questionnaires used in surveys among the adult population and some of the surveys among the adolescents have been sent by mail. Sometimes questionnaires used in youth studies have been administered to respondents in the classrooms of their respective schools, and were completed therein within a specific time limit. In recent years, it has been evident from all Icelandic surveys that response rates have been falling. This problem is not only attached to the alcohol and drug field surveys but also to surveys in other fields. This may be explained by increasingly negative attitudes towards the disclosure of information on private matters. Another explanation may be that too many surveys have been conducted, resulting in people becoming tired of such exercises.

In the survey supported by the Scandinavian Research Council in Criminology a telephone interview was used. This was the first national survey in the drug field to use this approach. This method has been widely used in order to survey attitudes (e.g. political attitudes) in recent years. Some problems were to be expected. It has been pointed out that this method is only realistic in the most industrialized countries with widespread telephone systems (Johnston 1980). Even in industrialized societies many households do not have telephones. It is questionable whether co-operation, trust and privacy can be established in a telephone interview when dealing with sensitive information such as drug use. These problems proved to have only minor relevance in this survey. A random sample was drawn, of whom 97.2 per cent had telephone numbers, and the final response rate was 70.5 per cent.

The results of this study may be compared with those from the survey which was conducted simultaneously by the Director General of Public Health, since both surveys were related to individuals aged 16 to 20 years. The outcomes of the two surveys showed a remarkable similarity.

The telephone interview has the advantage of being a quick and inexpensive procedure both for the researcher and the respondent. This method asks for less involvement from the respondents than the self-administered questionnaire, because they can answer directly over the telephone. This method also has limitations, since the questions cause a forced choice which almost always limits the answer to 'yes' or 'no'. Adolescents, or others, not able to answer in private cannot be expected to talk openly about sensitive issues while they are in the company of others (e.g. parents).

In general, conditions for epidemiological research in Iceland may be considered favourable. The National Register is kept up to date and it is relatively easy to trace individuals in a small country. In 1985 the Icelandic population was about 240 000. Sometimes it is even more advantageous to study the whole group than draw a sample. A study of mental disorders included all Icelanders belonging to a specific age cohort (Helgason 1964). And some medical studies have included all patients diagnosed with the disease to be studied, for example, epilepsy (Godmundsson 1966).

Despite these rather favourable conditions some problems have been evident as noted above. There is a temptation when conducting longitudinal studies to lengthen the questionnaire each time with additional items because of changes in the cultural context or changing research interests. It is a dilemma in comparative studies over a period, that one has to choose whether to learn from previous studies and progress towards better methods, or to preserve the original methods and not to lose comparability.

## Some Considerations on Future Actions

Low response rates have increased worries about the future prospects for conducting surveys in Iceland, and some other countries. Falling response rates reveal rather negative attitudes towards surveys among the general population. These matters must be taken into consideration, because, in spite of the shortcomings of surveys, no other method can possibly equal the comparability between one survey and another.

Most surveys on the use of alcohol and illegal drugs are carried out as *ad hoc* projects, and little attention is usually paid to comparability. Sometimes the researchers make only limited attempts to compare their findings with those from other studies. Often systematic comparison is left to the reader. In the future, single surveys will be conducted as before. Future action to improve comparability would involve moving from implicit to explicit comparison (Marsh 1967). When comparing surveys conducted in different settings additional information on the cultural context of the subject to be studied is often appreciated by the reader. It is also necessary to consider the whole research process. This includes data collection instruments, the content of the questions/interviews, field procedures, data preparation and data processing, and the data analysis to be applied.

Epidemiological research may become ossified if new research aspects and changing circumstances in the society are not considered. There may be two ways of conducting inter-societal research. The first one is to start with intra-societal comparability and then move towards inter-societal comparability. The second may lead directly to joint projects crossing national boundaries.

The Scandinavian Drinking Survey was developed the other way around. It started as a joint project, and when this was over, analysis was supposed to continue in each country. In this way national traditions could be further developed. Different research traditions are obvious in some of the published research reports, but the element of comparability is fully taken care of albeit in a different way.

The Scandinavian Drinking Survey confirms experiences from longitudinal studies, that a core of joint questions is needed, but such studies permit the adaptation, deletion and addition of questions at different times and in different settings. A common stock of questions, including items on frequency and quantity, that can be transformed into units of absolute alcohol in centilitres will make comparison easier. In this connection the different coverage rates among nations should be taken into account. The frequency of intoxication is also an important factor that is desirable to standardize, but involves further complications.

The same can be stated about the positive and negative consequences of drinking. Problem scales are more useful than an overall drinking score. Alcohol-related problems are culturally defined, but among related nations it may be possible to construct composite indices to cover specific problems.

Comparative cross national projects are usually rewarding exercises, and bring new experiences to national research traditions. They may be particularly important for nations with short histories of alcohol and drug research. Their drawbacks are that they are time consuming, and that unexpected problems may be discovered during the whole research process.

The spread of drug use among adolescents has been rapid throughout some populations because of current methods of communication and transportation. Accordingly, increased research activities should be supported also among nations in which drug surveys have not yet been conducted. Studies from other countries, specially neighbouring countries, are highly relevant. This, of course, increases the potential value of joint comparative research.

REFERENCES

Gudmundsson, G. (1966) 'Epilepsy in Iceland. A clinical and epidemiological investigation'. *Acta Neurologica Scandinavica*, Suppl. 25, vol. 43.
Hauge, R. and Irgens-Jensen, O. (1981a) *Scandinavian Drinking Survey:*

*Achieving comparability between surveys*

*Sampling Operations and Data Collections.* Reports from the National Institute for Alcohol Research, No. 44, Oslo: NIAR.

Hauge, R. and Irgens-Jensen, O. (1981b) *Scandinavian Drinking Survey: Demographic Variables and Representativeness of Samples.* Reports from the National Institute for Alcohol Research, No. 44, Oslo: NIAR.

Hauge, R. and Irgens-Jensen, O. (1984a) 'The relationship between alcohol consumption, alcohol intoxication and negative consequences of drinking in four Scandinavian countries', *British Journal of Addiction* 81, 513–24.

Hauge, R. and Irgens-Jensen, O. (1984b) *Use of Alcohol and the Negative Consequences of Such Use Among Men and Women in Four Nordic Countries.* Reports from the National Institute for Alcohol Research, No. 88, Oslo: NIAR.

Hauge, R. and Irgens-Jensen, O. (1986) *Age, Alcohol Consumption and the Experiencing of Negative Consequences of Drinking in Four Scandinavian Countries.* Reports from the National Institute for Alcohol Research, No. 3/86, Oslo: NIAR.

Helgason, T. (1964) 'Epidemiology of mental disorders in Iceland. A psychiatric and demographic investigation of 5395 Icelanders'. *Acta Psychiatrica Scandinavica*, Supp. 173.

Helgason, T. (1985) *Breytingar a neyslu afengis og fikniefna* (Changes in alcohol and drug use). Samband islenskra sveitarfelaga, Reykjavik. Radstefna um varnir gegn afengis- of fikniefnum 20. og 21. mai. Raoxtefnuskjal nr. 14.

Järvinen, M. and Ólafsdóttir, H. (1984) Nordiska Kvinnors dryckesmonster (Drinking patterns among nordic women), *Alcohol Policy-Journal of Nordic Alcohol Research*, Helsinki, vol. 1.4.

Järvenin, M. and Ólafsdóttir, H. (1986) Kvinnors dryckesmonster (Women's drinking pattern). In Järvinen, M. and Snare, A. (eds) *Kvinnor, Alkohol och Behandling* (*Women, Alcohol and Treatment*). NAD-Publikation Nr 13, Nordiska namnden for alkohol- och drogforskning, Helsinki.

Johnston, L.D. (1980) *Review of General Population Surveys of Drug Abuse.* WHO Offset Publication No. 52, Geneva; WHO.

Kristmundsson, O. (1985) *Olögleg avana- og fikniefni a Islandi* (Illicit drugs in Iceland), Ryekjavik: Doms- og kirkjumalaöuneytio.

Marsh, R.M. (1967) *Comparative Sociology*, New York: Harcourt, Brace and World.

Mäkelä, K. (1981) *Scandinavian Drinking Survey: Construction of Composite Indices of Drinking Attitudes and Personal Experiences Related to Drinking.* Reports from the National Institute for Alcohol Research, No. 47, Oslo: NIAR.

Mäkelä, K. (1982) *Permissible Starting Age for Drinking in Four Scandinavian Countries.* Reports from the National Institute for Alcohol Research, No. 77, Oslo: NIAR.

Mäkelä, K. (1984) *Attitudes Towards Drinking and Drunkenness in Four Scandinavian Countries.* Reports from the National Institute for Alcohol Research, No. 77, Oslo: NIAR.

Ragnarsdottir Briem, G. (1981) *En Enkätundersökning – alkoholvanor bland isländsk skolungdom 1980 – om forandringar i alkoholvanor bland isländsk skolungdom under 1970 talet* (A survey – on drinking pattern among Icelandic students 1980 – on the changes in alcohol pattern among Icelandic students in the 1970s), Linköpings Universitet: Sociologi C-1, vt.

Simpura, J. (1981) *Scandinavian Drinking Survey: Construction of Indices of Alcohol Intake.* Reports from the National Institute for Alcohol

Research, No. 46, Oslo: NIAR.

Simpura, J. (1985a) *The Optimal Classification of Annual Alcohol Consumption in the Scandinavian Drinking Survey*. Reports from the National Institute for Alcohol Research, No. 1/85, Oslo: NIAR.

Simpura, J. (1985b) *Results on the Relationship Between the Level of Alcohol Consumption and the Shape of Consumption Distribution by Sex and Age in the Four Scandinavian Countries. A Data Report*. Reports from the National Institutes for Alcohol Research, No. 3/85, Oslo: NIAR.

Simpura, J. (1985c) *Composition of Extreme Populations with Respect to Drinking: Abstainers and the Lightest and the Heaviest Drinkers in Four Nordic Countries*. Reports from the National Institute for Alcohol Research, No. 6/85, Oslo: NIAR.

Simpura, J. (1985d) *Beverage Specific Drinking Patterns in Four Nordic Countries*. Reports from the National Institute for Alcohol Research, No. 7/85, Oslo: NIAR.

Smart, R.G. and Murray, G.F. (1981) 'Review of trends in alcohol and cannabis use among young people', *Bulletin on Narcotics* 33, 4, 77–90.

# 5. The Problems and Logistics of Alcohol Research in Different Settings: The Example of the USSR

IRINA ANOKHINA and NIKOLAI IVANETS

*Abstract.* This review highlights some of the problems and logistics of carrying out surveys of alcohol use and misuse in different cultural and social contexts. This suggests that the future conduct of surveys in different settings is likely to be greatly aided by general acceptance of common definitions and methods in relation to 'key' issues. This view is elaborated on the basis of clinical practice and alcohol research in the USSR, a huge and diverse country, containing 280 million people.

## Introduction

The increase in scientific studies into the use and misuse of alcohol has highlighted the problems of devising truly comparable measures by which data may be recorded. This issue is of crucial importance in relation to the monitoring of the extent of alcohol use and misuse, both within single countries and on an international basis.

Information indicating the patterns of alcohol misuse is available from a number of different sources. These include specially designed studies such as population surveys, together with data routinely gathered by a variety of health and social service agencies. Such data frequently produce conflicting results and are also often based upon quite discrepant procedures. Accordingly, much potentially useful evidence is unsuitable for regional or international comparisons. At best such information serves to indicate trends within a single locality or country.

The USSR, with about 280 million people, contains huge regions which vary substantially from each other in relation to their geographical, ethnic, economic, cultural and genetic characteristics. These regions encompass a wide variety of

46

drinking styles involving different types of alcoholic beverage. In consequence the USSR provides a useful model whereby researchers may attempt to adopt methods which produce dependable comparative evidence about alcohol-related problems.

Epidemiological studies in various regions of the USSR have indicated that comparable results need to be based upon relatively uniform research procedures. The latter need not be unduly rigid but should at least be based upon agreed general principles and definitions.

## THE DEFINITION OF ALCOHOL DEPENDENCE

The production of acceptable comparative information necessitates the creation of a common form of reference and agreement upon basic concepts. Past endeavours have certainly been impeded by the lack of a generally accepted operational definition of 'alcoholism' or alcohol-related problems. In consequence epidemiological studies have applied varied and sometimes incompatible criteria. This variety has failed to generate a uniform set of diagnostic criteria for clinical use or for survey purposes. The lack of such criteria may have inhibited both the early recognition of problem drinkers and the effective implementation of strategies to prevent alcohol misuse.

The scientific literature contains a confusing profusion of terms such as 'alcoholism', 'chronic alcohol intoxication', 'problem drinking' and 'alcohol abuse'. Such terms have rather different meanings and reflect a variety of factors. These include the clinical features of the alcohol dependence syndrome, the social correlates of alcohol misuse in general and social responses to the harmful use of alcohol. It is difficult for a general definition to take due account of such a multiplicity of considerations. Moreover, the different interpretations to which specific definitions are subjected hinders the establishment of a widely acceptable scientific classification of alcohol dependence and its sequelae.

## CLASSIFICATIONS OF ALCOHOL DEPENDENCE

Several distinctive methods of classifying alcohol dependence currently co-exist in the USSR. The precise perspective adopted depends on the individual's requirements, on the purpose and scope of specific research activities and on the profession or scientific discipline (e.g. lawyer, medical practitioner, sociologist).

Jellinek's well-known classification of alcohol dependence into five subgroups (alpha, beta, gamma, delta and epsilon) is widely adopted (Jellinek 1960). Many clinicians in the USSR employ a three-fold classification of alcohol dependence. Portnov and Pyatnitskaya (1973) have elaborated an approach to alcohol dependence which takes account of both the severity of physical dependence and the extent of psychological effects. The initial stage is referred to as 'neurasthenic'. This involves psychological dependence on alcohol, increased tolerance and transition from episodic to regular alcohol use. The second, intermediate, level of dependence or 'narcomaniac' phase, is characterized by physical dependence, increased craving, modified patterns of intoxication, maximum tolerance, 'pseudo bout drinking' and marked alcohol-related personality changes. The third or 'terminal' phase involves decreased tolerance, the development of bout drinking, dementia and (often) alcohol psychosis.

An earlier approach by Strelchuk (1966) grouped such symptoms in a slightly different way. This classification is based upon a 'syndrome of pathologically changed responses to alcohol'. This includes craving and loss of control. Strelchuk indicated that other symptoms were less specific. The early stage of alcohol dependence is characterized by increased tolerance, frequency of amnesias linked with intoxication and alcohol overdose. The intermediate stage of alcohol dependence involves withdrawal symptoms following cessation of drinking, maximum tolerance to alcohol and adverse social and psychological consequences. The third or 'severe' stage involves decreased tolerance and even 'intolerance' to alcohol, intoxication-related amnesia after consuming relatively small levels of alcohol, disorders of the central nervous system and frequent alcohol psychoses. These classifications, together with those most often used both in the USSR and elsewhere, provide a basis for a commonly adaptable international classification. The adoption of such a unified approach would greatly assist the collection of comparable clinical and general population data related to alcohol dependence.

A number of different criteria exist whereby alcohol-related problems may be discussed or assessed. These include clinical and biological factors as well as social and cultural ones. In the USSR 'alcohol dependence' is widely perceived as a progressive condition characterized by both psychological and physical dependence and by the onset of withdrawal symptoms upon the cessation of drinking. In its extreme form, as elaborated by Edwards *et al.*

48

(1977), the alcohol dependence syndrome is accompanied by persistent neurological disorders and psychological impairment. Alcohol dependence is invariably accompanied by a constellation of adverse social consequences which afflict both the dependent drinker and society at large.

The conceptualization of generally acceptable diagnostic criteria for alcohol dependence is of great importance in relation to assessing the extent of this condition. Such a broad agreement is also a necessary prerequisite for international comparative studies. Even so, the majority of suggested classifications suffer from specific limitations. Clinical evidence produced within the USSR (Strelchuk 1973, Ivanets, Igonon 1983, Ivanets, Anokhina 1984, Ivanets, Manshikova 1984) indicates that these are separate and distinctive clinical types of alcohol dependence. They are characterized by peculiarities in their development, course, prognosis and in relation to the appropriate preventive strategy and clinical response. A full delineation should encompass both the severity of dependence, together with a more wide-ranging elaboration of the different forms of adverse alcohol-related consequences. The latter are often associated with excessive or inappropriate drinking which does not involve dependence. Such information is required in order to arrive at an adequate clinical assessment, and in order to guide the appropriate therapeutic responses.

Both Soviet and other authors have suggested a variety of criteria in order to distinguish between alcohol dependence and more general indicators of alcohol misuse. Some investigators have emphasized clinical symptoms as the major diagnostic factors. These include changes in tolerance, disappearance of the vomiting reflex, the onset of amnesias and hangover symptoms (Zhislin 1935, Strelchuk 1956, Portnov and Fedotov 1965), frequency of alcohol consumption (Mayer-Gross, Slater and Roth 1954) and personality changes. Other investigators have asserted that one or two diagnostic criteria are insufficient. Only an extensive array of biological processes provides an adequate basis for clinical assessment (Portnov and Pyatnitskaya 1973).

The validity of a clinical assessment is certainly enhanced if an 'integrated approach' is adopted which pays due attention to medical, social and other factors. Alcohol-related consequences, such as accidents, social, family and public order problems, are far more widespread than is 'alcohol dependence', however defined. Even so, a generally accepted method of distinguishing between alcohol dependence and the inappropriate or 'problematic' use of alcohol has not emerged in the USSR. The confusion between clinical alcohol dependence and other forms of alcohol misuse has led to wide variations in the levels of 'alcohol misuse' and 'alcohol dependence' reported by researchers, even when describing the same localities or communities. Such variation is also evident in other countries in which efforts have been made to assess the extent of alcohol misuse. Clinical studies of problem drinkers have indicated the existence of six variations of the alcohol withdrawal syndrome as well as six types of alcohol abuse, each one of which is associated with a specific form of craving for alcohol (Kachajev *et al.* 1986, Valentik 1984, Ivanets, Valentik 1984).

During recent years clinical studies have widely applied epidemiological approaches to alcohol-related problems. In such investigations the researchers have examined identified problem drinkers and people who are at high risk of becoming heavy drinkers or alcohol dependents. The latter subgroup have been identified in the context of studies of variations within the general population (Urakov and Kulikaov 1977, Kachajev and Urakov 1979, Hagnet *et al.* (1986).

Views differ upon the diagnostic criteria for alcohol dependence, and at present many diagnostic approaches coexist. In order to arrive at a full and adequate assessment due account should be taken of clinical, social, psychological and biological (laboratory) evidence. It is widely accepted that craving for alcohol is the hallmark of the alcohol dependence syndrome.

## Evaluating the Effectiveness of Treatment

The evaluation of therapeutic approaches to alcohol dependence is of great importance. Many similarities are evident between the main treatment approaches available in different countries, even though there is variation in emphasis and the relative popularity of different philosophies and methods.

It is extremely difficult to reach overall conclusions about the 'effectiveness' of specific therapeutic approaches obtained in different countries. As in other types of alcohol research a variety of methods and criteria have been employed in past attempts to evaluate treatment outcomes. In some countries assessments have been based upon the follow-up of patients over several years or simply over a few months (Polich, Armor and Braiker 1981, Heather and Robertson 1986, Vaillant 1983). In order to attain a uniform approach to treatment assessment a standard outcome period of five years has been established in the USSR. During this time the alcohol dependent patient must completely abstain from the use of alcohol in order to be removed from the registry of the clinic. Total abstinence is generally accepted as the hallmark of remission from alcohol dependence in the USSR. The assessment of treatment effectiveness, like most other things in the alcohol field, is massively influenced by the criteria and methods used by researchers and clinicians.

## IDENTIFICATION OF PROBLEM DRINKERS

The choice of methods again emerges as a key issue when considering evidence about the nature and extent of alcohol-related problems in the general population. A constructive approach to the prevention of alcohol misuse is most likely to be effective if policy makers are equipped with adequate information about the levels and trends in various forms of alcohol problems. This information should not be confined to alcohol dependence, but should encompass the general spectrum of social, public order, family and other problems associated with excessive or inappropriate drinking. In the USSR a number of strategies have been adopted in order to assess the scale of such misuse. Similar data are needed to assess the use and misuse of both prescribed and illegal drugs. As noted in Chapters 1 and 2 the latter are especially difficult to examine.

It is a basic epidemiological problem that very often the alleged level of alcohol problems is a reflection of the provision of services for such problems rather than a measure of alcohol misuse in the community. A specialized system of health care provision for problem drinkers has been established in the USSR. As noted above, the operation of this system is assisted by a broad, if not total, agreement upon basic diagnostic criteria and methods of assessing therapeutic outcome.

The variation in health service provision is not the sole reason for divergent indices of alcohol misuse in different regions or countries. Social, cultural, economic and demographic factors combine to exert important influences upon such indices.

Within the USSR considerable regional variations are evident in relation to patterns of alcohol production and consumption (including beverage preferences). Such regional differences are compounded by ethnic and national traditions. The scale of these variations is exemplified in the Soviet context by comparing evidence from the Baltic and Caucasian Republics. In 1980 the highest officially recorded rate of alcohol dependence in the USSR (in the Latvian Soviet Federal Republic) was seven times greater than in the lowest one (the Armenian Soviet Federal Republic) (Urakov, Tvorogova and Miroshnichenko 1983). It is emphasized that the Latvian and Armenian republics differ markedly from each other in relation to their ethnic composition, population density, urban-rural balance, degree of industrialization, climate, geographical features, customs, traditions, patterns and levels of alcohol production and consumption and the numbers of residents who have migrated from other areas of the USSR.

## CONDUCTING COMPARATIVE STUDIES

Clinical/epidemiological studies in specific geographical areas, employing cross-sectional sampling methods, facilitate the collection of representative data. These provide an invaluable profile of the social-demographic, economic and cultural characteristics of the study area. Population studies of this type identify a constellation of questions and factors related to the aetiology, development and changing pattern of alcohol-related problems in different communities.

While such studies have great value, it should be noted that comparative investigations which attempt to cover several countries are beset by major problems allied to the varied nature of data elicited in different settings. Definitions and research methodologies vary considerably in different countries. Such differences present major problems for the conduct of comparative studies or the attainment of general conclusions about the use and misuse of alcohol.

Standardized research procedures are necessary in order to obtain truly comparable data. In the context of surveys this requires the use of uniform instruments (e.g. interview schedules and questionnaires). Such instruments would reduce the variations currently attributable to widely disparate research approaches.

A uniform methodology is attainable, but has to be applied in varied settings. Specific studies have to be designed in the context of regional peculiarities.

During the past decade the use of comparative methods has expanded and has generated an extensive array of information (Petrakov 1972, Solms 1974).

One result of this activity is that research methods have become more robust and sophisticated.

The increase in comparative studies has been attributable to a rising demand for indicators of the regional variation of alcohol misuse. This type of information is also necessary in order to establish regularities of the development, features and consequences (both medical and social) of the alcohol dependence syndrome and of alcohol misuse in general. In addition, only comparative studies are able to investigate or to clarify the relationship between alcohol and misuse and a host of environmental variables. These include social and demographic, economic, occupational, climatic, geographical, ethnic and cultural factors. Such factors have widely varied influences. Accordingly it is necessary to establish the levels and directions of association between specific factors as well as monitoring their quantitative and qualitative features. The role of any single factor is likely to vary in different contexts according to the cultural setting.

The nature and extent of regional differences in the use and misuse of alcohol have to be monitored if service provision is to be adequately planned and evaluated. General population surveys, as well as clinical studies, have an invaluable role in this context.

## Conclusion

Available evidence and past experience suggest a number of practical ways of improving the comparability of data related to alcohol use and misuse in different settings. These include the elaboration and adoption of a single set of definitions of alcohol (and drug) dependence and of allied concepts such as 'remission'. In addition, the acceptance of uniform methods of assessing treatment outcomes would be a major asset to future comparisons of therapeutic effectiveness. Such standardization would be of great value both to clinical studies and to general population surveys. A set of generally acceptable minimum criteria for research and clinical practice is required to guide future comparative studies. Such criteria need to be illustrated by examples from existing research results related to epidemiological and preventive work. Future data collection should be organised in accord with these criteria. In addition, information collected on this basis should be accessible by right to all legitimate specialist researchers and clinicians. Similar conclusions are relevant to studies of other psychoactive substances such as illegal drugs. In many respects epidemiological studies related to alcohol are better developed than those related to illegal drugs, and may serve as a model for the latter.

The creation of such a standard set of procedures and criteria is a necessary prerequisite for acceptable comparative research. This step will need the active co-operation of researchers, clinicians and policy makers from all potential participating countries.

REFERENCES

Edwards, G., Gross, M.M. and Keller, M., et al. (1977) Alcohol-Related Disabilities. WHO Offset Publication No. 32. Geneva: WHO.

Hagnell, O., Lanke, J. and Rorsman, B. (1986) 'Predictors of alcoholism in the Lundby study', *European Archives of Psychiatry and Neurological Sciences*, 235: 187–199.

Heather, B.B. and Robertson, I. (1986) *Controlled Drinking*, London: Methuen.

Ivanets, N.N. (1985) 'Klinicheckiye varianty alcogoloizma', In: *5 Vserossiysky sjezd nevropatologov i psikhiatrov, Tezisy dokladov*, Moskva, t.2., 54–55.

Ivanets, N.N. and Anokhina, I.P. (1984) 'O nekotorykh konstitutsionalnobiologichechikh factorakh, opredelyayuschikh skorost formirovaniya alkogolizma', *7 sjezd neuropatologov i psikhiatrov Ukrainskoi SSR 19–21 September 1984, Tzisy dokladov*, part 1, Vinnitsa, 130–131.

Ivanets, N.N. and Igonon, A.L. (1983) 'Klinika alcogolisma', In: G.V. Morozov, B.E. Konanova, E.A. Babajan (eds) *Alcoholizm* (Rukovodstvo dlya vrachei) Moskva, Meditsina, 75–149.

Ivanets, N.N. and Manshikova, E.S. (1984) 'Nekotoriye Klinico-patageneticheskiye zakonomernosti alkogolizma', in: G.V. Morozov (ed) *Klinicheskiye osnoviy alkogolizma (sbornik nauchnikh trudov)* 3–10, Mockva.

Ivanets, N.N. and Valentik, V.V. (1984) 'K kharakteristike osnovnikh klinicheskikh variantov pervichnogo patologicheskogo vlechenija k alcogolu', In: *Aktualnyje voprosy narcologii. Tezisy dokladou Vsesojuznogo simpoziuma psikhiatrov. Dushanbe 25–27 sentyabrya 1984*, Dushanbe, 81–83.

Jellinek, E.M. (1960) *The Disease Concept of Alcoholism*, New Jersey: Hillhouse.

Kachajev, A.K., Ivanets, N.N., Igonin, A.L., Urakov, I.G. and Shumskij, N.G. (1986) *Glossarij*, "Standaritzonannyje psikhopatologicheskije simptomy i sindromy dlja unifitsirovannoj klinicheskoj otesenki alkogolizma i alcogolnykh psikhozov (metodicheskije recomendatsyj) 'MZ SSR, Upravlenije po vnedreniju novykh lekarstvennykh sredstv i meditsynskoj tekhniki, Moskva, 63.

Kachjev, A.K. and Urakov, I.G. (1979) 'Sravnitelnyj analiz uchtennykh pokazatelej i rezultatov epidemiologicheskogo issledovanija populatsiji "sploshnym" metodom v otsenke rasprostranennosti pjanstva i alkogolisma', In: *Alkogolizm. Aktualnyje voprosy kliniki, patogeneza i terapiji alkogolnikh zabolevanij*, Dushanbe, 137–151.

Mayer-Gross, W., Slater, E. and Roth, M. (1954) *Clinical Psychiatry*, London:

Petrakou, B.D. (1972) 'Psikhicheskaja zabolevajemost v nekotorykh stranakh v XX veke/*Sotsialno-gigienicheskoje Issledovanije*, Moskva, Meditsina, 300.

Polich, J., Armor, D. and Braiker, H. (1981) *The Course of Alcoholism: 4 Years After Treatment*, New York: Wiley.

Portnov, A.A. and Fedotov, D.D. (1956) *Psychiatry*, Moscow: Medicine.
Portnov, A.A. and Pyatnitskaya, I.H. (1973) *Klinika Alkogolizma*, Leningrad: Medicine.
Solms, H. (1974) 'Alkogolizm in Europe', In: *Work in Progress on Alcoholism*, Ann. N.Y. Acad. Sci., v. 273, WHO, STR, 24–32.
Strelchuk, I.V. (1956) *Klinika i Lechenije Narkomanii*, Moscow: Medhize.
Strelchuk, I.V. (1966) *Ostrajia i Hronicheskaja Intoksikacija Alkogolem*, Moscow: Medicine.
Strelchuk, I.V. (1973) *Ostraja i khronocheskaja intoksikatsija alkogolem*, izdanije 2, dopolnenoje, Meditsina, 384.
Urakov, I.A. and Kulikov, V.V., (1977) *Chronicheskij alkogolizm*, Meditsina, 165.
Urakov, I.G., Tvorogova, N.A. and Miroshnichenko, L.D. (1983) *Dinamika iosnovnyje Tendencii Izmenenija Struktury Vyjavlennyh Kontingentov Bolnhy Alkogolizmom (1976–1978)*, v kn.: Voprosy Kliniki, Diagnostiki i Profilaktiki Alkogolisma i Narkomanii, Moscow: Medicine.
Vaillant, G.E. (1983) *The Natural History of Alcoholism*, Cambridge, Mass.: Harvard University Press.
Valentik, Y.V. (1984) 'Klinicheskije varianty aktualizatsyji patologicheskogo vlechenija k alkogolju i bolnykh alkogolizmom', In: *7 sjezd neuropatologov i psikhiatrov Ukrainskoj SSR. Tezisy dokladov*, Vinnitsa 117–118.
Zhislin, S.G. (1935) *Ob Alkoholnyh Rasstrojistvah*, Voronej: Kommuna.

# 6. The USSR: Relevance for Research and Policy

MARTIN PLANT

The USSR, as a huge and populous country, provides a wealth of excellent experience in relation to the conduct of comparative research into alcohol and other psychoactive drugs. The review by Drs Anokhina and Ivanets indicates that scientific thinking in the USSR is characterized by both a wide level of agreement with that in other European countries and by some differences in emphasis. Both authors stress the value of devising and adopting generally acceptable working definitions and research approaches in order to advance comparative studies of alcohol use and misuse. They indicate that a fairly clear delineation of alcohol dependence or 'alcoholism' has been accomplished within the USSR. This is broadly compatible with the classic formulation of Jellinek (1960). Even so, researchers in some countries would give greater emphasis to the fact that alcohol-related problems cover a much wider range of consequences than those associated with alcohol dependence. Many of the adverse consequences associated with drinking do not involve dependence, but are associated with inappropriate drinking that is acute rather than chronic. For example, a host of accidents, social and law enforcement problems are linked to intoxication. The latter is especially commonplace amongst young males and is most likely to be connected with drinking 'sprees' during weekends (Edwards, Gross, Keller, Moser and Room 1977, Collins 1982, Ross 1984, Royal College of Psychiatrists 1986). Accordingly, comparative research into alcohol use and misuse needs to go beyond either clinical studies or attempts to measure the prevalence of 'alcoholism' in the general population. As indicated in Chapters 1 and 2, and elsewhere in this book, future research should attempt a rather wider task, namely, the measurement of patterns of both alcohol use and alcohol-related consequences in the general population. The conceptualization of 'alcoholism' as a disease is not simply a Soviet perspective. It is shared by many people in the alcohol field and is particularly influential in North America. It is emphasized that some researchers, while acknowledging the importance of alcohol dependence, have attempted to present a broader conceptualization which also encompasses the non-dependent abuse of alcohol, and which, in some cases, suggests a variety of therapeutic objectives and responses (Heather and Robertson 1986).

Drs Anokhina and Ivanets highlight a major theme which is noted throughout this book: Indices whereby alcohol-related problems may be measured are, individually, highly imperfect. Even when data are available from 'official agencies' and other sources, they are biased and flawed by variations in local, regional and national methods of definition and application. Accordingly, even within a single country it is frequently difficult to attain a 'standardized' set of measures of the use and misuse of legal or illicit drugs. Chapter 5 highlights a number of clinical and epidemiological problems associated with alcohol misuse. Similar difficulties could equally be identified in relation to tobacco, prescribed and illicit drugs. As noted by Anokhina, Ivanets, Garretsen and other contributors to this book, survey work in relation to such substances is generally far less well developed. It is hoped that in future research into the use and misuse of psychoactive substances other than alcohol will benefit from awareness of the many practical problems which beset current work in this field.

**REFERENCES**

Collins, J.J. (jun.)(ed)(1982) *Drinking and Crime*, London: Tavistock.
Edwards, G., Gross, M.M., Keller, J. and Room, R. (1977) *Alcohol-Related Disabilities*. WHO Offset Publications No. 32, Geneva: WHO.
Heather, N. and Robertson, I. (1986) *Problem Drinking*, Harmondsworth, Middx.: Penguin.
Jellinek, E.M. (1960) *The Disease Concept of Alcoholism*, New Haven, Conn.: Hillhouse.
Ross, H.L. (1984) *Deterring the Drinking Driver*, Lexington, Mass.: Lexington Books.
Royal College of Psychiatrists (1986) *Alcohol: Our Favourite Drug*, London: Tavistock.

# 7. The Measurement of Problems in Community Surveys

HENK F.L. GARRETSEN

## Abstract

It is argued that community surveys are useful in measuring problems related to alcohol and other psychoactive drugs such as minor tranquillizers and sedatives. However, it is recognized that the survey method has limitations. Several difficulties are identified. Population surveys are, however, much better able to handle some sorts of problems than others. In general, such surveys are less well suited to the assessment of problems related to illicit drugtaking.

In this review the main emphasis is placed upon alcohol surveys. The topics discussed include the usefulness of surveys compared with some other methods, the limitations of the survey method, the measurement of alcohol-related problems, the interrelations between such problems and overall problems scores. Less attention is paid to the measurement of problems related to other drugs. As noted elsewhere in this book, far more European research has been conducted into alcohol than into illegal drugs. It is emphasized that most of the themes highlighted in this chapter are as relevant to drug surveys as they are to alcohol surveys.

## Introduction

This review discusses the measurement of problems, related both to alcohol and to other psychoactive drugs, in community surveys.

In a survey, information is gathered from a population sample or other study group in a systematic way by questionnaires and interview schedules. Several methods of data collection may be used. It is, for instance, possible to interview respondents face to face at home, by telephone, in the street, school, workplace or in other locations either directly or by a self-completed questionnaire. The latter may be presented in person by fieldworkers or may be sent to respondents by mail. Most surveys elicit information from representative samples of individuals, but samples may consist of families or households.

Problems associated with the use of alcohol and other psychoactive drugs may fruitfully be examined by surveys. The use of this method raises several important questions: Is the survey the best approach? What limitations may be distinguished? Which types of alcohol/drug-related problems may be measured? This chapter considers such issues and the key question of how surveys might attempt to measure the use of alcohol and of other psychoactive drugs. This review is mainly concerned with surveys of alcohol use and misuse. The topics covered include the merits of surveys in comparison with other methods, the measurement of alcohol-related problems by surveys and the interrelations between specific alcohol-related problems and overall problem scores. Less emphasis is placed upon the measurement of problems associated with other forms of psychoactive substance. A distinction is made between legal and illicit drug use, and this review is concluded with a brief discussion of the future direction of survey research.

## THE MEASUREMENT OF DRINKING PROBLEMS

### The Survey in Comparison with Other Methods

The survey method can be used to estimate the numbers of 'excessive' drinkers and 'problem' drinkers by measuring drinking behaviour and alcohol-related problems. Other methods are used, especially to estimate the number of excessive drinkers, or 'alcoholics'. The 'Ledermann Formula' has been widely applied as a method of attempting to estimate the number of 'excessive' drinkers. According to Ledermann the distribution of alcohol consumption in a population approximates to a 'one parameter log normal distribution', the one parameter being *per capita* alcohol consumption (Ledermann 1956, Knibbe, Drop, van Reek and Saenger 1985).

Other methods of estimating the number of 'alcoholics' or problem drinkers in a society are based upon mortality figures ascribed to alcoholism/alcohol dependence, or upon those related to suicide and/or liver cirrhosis (e.g. Jellinek 1960).

A few other methods which estimate the number of 'alcoholics' and which are also based on statistical information are sporadically used (Walsh and Walsh 1973). These include estimations based on the number of admissions to general and/or psychiatric hospitals and to alcohol clinics for people with alcohol-related problems, the number of convictions due to drunkenness or driving under the influence of alcohol and the number of traffic accidents associated with alcohol use.

All of the above methods have one or more distinct disadvantages: The practical application of such data is uncertain, estimates are dependent on the accuracy of the statistical records on which they are based, and such data have questionable validity.

In comparison with the above methods, surveys have some clear merits. The prevalence of (excessive) drinking can be measured among various subpopulations and it is possible to apply different criteria. Furthermore, many factors which are related to drinking can be examined. Finally, the survey is particularly useful in measuring drinking problems in the community and among specific subgroups.

## Some Limitations of the Survey Method

The validity of survey results depends on a number of factors. In general, the survey must meet the standards that are routinely required of social scientific and epidemiological research – demands concerning the random sample, the interview technique and the analysis. The items included in the questionnaire must be good indicators of the topics under study, such as the use of alcohol (and drugs) and related problems. Apart from the quality of the instrument itself, it is unclear to what extent survey data can be regarded as reliable (consistent) and valid (accurate). The main problem is that inherent in such data is the *underestimation* of reported alcohol consumption and related problems. Such under-reporting is almost certainly a greater problem in relation to illicit drug use.

When survey data are compared with sales data, a coverage of only 20 to 70 per cent has been found (Pernanen 1974, Knibbe *et al.* 1985). In three Dutch surveys a coverage of 49, 48 and 44 per cent respectively was evident in 1958, 1970 and 1981. It is conceivable that underestimation occurs because excessive drinkers and problem drinkers are less readily willing to take part in a survey or that in an interview they consciously or unconsciously (partly) deny their drinking and alcohol-related problems (Mulder and Garretsen 1983, Garretsen 1984, Garretsen 1985). Under-reporting may also involve people who do not drink heavily or who simply forget how much they have consumed (Philipsen, Knibbe and van Reek 1983). In some localities under-reporting may vary within different subgroups. Thus a survey of drinking habits in Rotterdam indicated that, from a comparison of self-reports and spouse reports, women underestimated the 'frequency of drinking six glasses or more' more often than did men (Garretsen 1983, 1985). In general it can be noted that underestimation is higher for illegal than for legal drugs. Warner (1979) has noted that tobacco surveys detect only about 75 per cent of cigarette sales, compared with about 90 per cent ten years earlier, when smoking incurred less stigma.

The survey method is still useful as long as its limitations are duly noted. It is desirable to anticipate underestimation of drinking behaviour and drinking problems as much as possible; for instance, by confronting respondents with both general as well as specific questions. However, it is clear that underestimation cannot be entirely prevented. Therefore, if possible, it may in some cases be desirable to determine the extent of this form of bias.

With regard to the unintended under-reporting of consumption (forgetting) the diary method may be very useful (Poikolainen and Karkkainen 1983). It is possible to ascertain, to some extent, the proportion of problem drinkers who cooperate with surveys and who report fully about their problems. The methods available to clarify this key issue include the following:

- interviewing partners of respondents or other significant persons about the drinking behaviour and drinking problems of these people (Garretsen 1984, Leonard, Dunn and Jacob 1983).
- comparison of answers provided by the respondents with data of official registers (i.e. hospitals, other service agencies, etc.)- (Mulder and Garretsen 1983).
- stratifying the sample by persons who are, or have been, identified in the past as problem drinkers (Mulford and Wilson 1966).

Each method had its own distinct disadvantages, and in some cases important issues of privacy are involved (Garretsen 1984).

### Drinking Problems Measured in Surveys

Any problem (for the drinker or for others) closely connected with drinking constitutes a drinking problem. Of course a subjective element plays a role in defining what constitutes an alcohol (or drug) related problem. Some drinking problems are more dose-related than others; for instance, liver damage is more likely to be associated with prolonged heavy drinking; this is not necessarily the case for the so-called 'social problems'.

Which sorts of drinking problems are commonly dealt with in surveys? Surveys have been used to examine a variety of variables. A survey by Cahalan (1976) distinguished the following eleven problems: Frequent intoxication; binge drinking; symptomatic drinking (loss of control and physical dependence); escape drinking (psychological dependence); problems with spouse or relatives; problems with friends or neighbours; problems at work; problems with the law/accidents; health problems; financial problems; belligerence.

Some problems have been measured by a scale consisting of several items, others by a single question.

In some studies different drinking problems have been combined into separate 'dimensions'. For instance, in two identical surveys carried out in the Netherlands, five 'dimensions' – five types of alcohol-related problems – were distinguished, to a large extent based on Cahalan's approach (Garretsen and Knibbe 1985). These were:

- Psychological dependency, measured by eight items which show enough 'internal consistency' to use as a scale (according to the Statistical Package for the Social Sciences (SPSS) program 'Reliability', the coefficient Cronbach's Alpha has been measured and appeared to be about 0.80). Among others, the following items have been included: 'a drink is helpful to forget one's worries' and 'a drink is needed when one is tense or nervous'.
- Symptomatic drinking, also measured by an internally consistent scale of eight items, such as 'having difficulty stopping drinking' and 'black-outs'.
- Social problems divided into six sub-categories: Problems with partners or relatives; problems with friends or neighbours; job problems; problems with law or police; relatives or friends complaining about financial affairs and relatives or friends complaining about aggressive behaviour by respondents. Some problems have been measured by one question, other problems by more.
- Health problems or accidents. Accidents have been measured by one question, health problems by a few items (in hospital

because of drinking, the respondent feeling that drinking has been harmful to his or her health, and a physician has discussed respondent's drinking).

- Frequent intoxication/hangover has been measured by two questions with a number of precoded categories.

It is very important to recognize that surveys are much better suited to examining some sorts of drinking problems than others. In the first place, many drinking problems exist more at social than at individual levels and are not easily measured in individual interviews. An example of this is loss of production because of drinking (Room 1977).

It is, however, questionable to what extent the omission of some indicators (like cirrhosis) may lead to incorrect estimates of the number of individuals with drinking problems.

### Interrelations Between Drinking Problems and Overall Problem Scores

The extent to which different drinking problems are interconnected has been examined in several studies.

Vaillant, Gale and Milofsky (1982) compared different problem indicators, including those of clinical and behavioural problems, and concluded that these two sets of criteria largely identify the same people as problem drinkers. But, in a Dutch study, three types of problem drinking were distinguished. It was concluded that it appeared likely that one type will not be detected by survey-research, namely, that characterized by the occurrence of cirrhosis but not involving other types of alcohol problems (Peters 1982).

Room (1977) concluded from a review of the literature that: 'in the general population of the USA, having any particular drinking problem is only a modest predictor of having any other particular problem, and having a problem at one particular time is only a modest predictor of having the same problem at another time'.

The interrelations of different drinking problems have also been studied in the two surveys in the Netherlands (in the City of Rotterdam and in the province of Limburg). For the five types of drinking problems distinguished intercorrelations were computed (Garretsen and Knibbe 1984). The correlations ranged from 0.20 to 0.61; all were significant but were not high enough to confirm that two or more problems quite often occurred at the same time. The highest correlations were found between 'social problems' and 'symptomatic drinking' (0.61 in Rotterdam and 0.56 in Limburg).

It seems that phenomena measured by 'symptomatic drinking', such as 'loss of control' and blackouts, were least acceptable to other people and so caused 'social problems'. The result of this was that all correlations were significant, but modest. This means perhaps that the research distinction between different problem areas was meaningful and that these areas together may have provided a good indication of the variety and extent of drinking problems.

Sometimes it may be useful to construct an overall score of 'problem drinking' on the basis of separate adverse consequences. In the two Dutch surveys cited above 'problem drinking' was defined as 'excessive alcohol consumption which is connected with physical, psychological or social problems for the problem drinker him or herself or for others', and one variable, 'problem drinking', has been constructed on the basis of the drinking problems experienced and the amount drunk. As noted above, the Dutch surveys were largely based on the work of Cahalan (1976) in the USA. Cahalan also constructed an overall problem score. Many studies have used such scores for certain types of alcohol-related problems.

However, as Room (1977) has pointed out, little attention has been paid to the methods of aggregation used (such as the problems of weighting different drinking problems or ranking them in some order of severity). An overall score of problem drinking may be convenient to produce an overall view of the prevalence of alcohol problems in different geographical areas or in various subpopulations. On the other hand it has to be recognized that such aggregation blurs some individual details. It may often be better to study drinking problems separately.

## THE MEASUREMENT OF PROBLEMS RELATED TO THE USE OF OTHER DRUGS

Surveys have been related to legal drugs, especially alcohol, far more often than to illicit drugs. The following section presents a brief discussion of the application of surveys to drugs other than alcohol.

*Legal Drug Use.* 'Legal drugs' include, tea, coffee, tobacco and prescribed drugs such as tranquillizers and anti-depressants. The recreational use of glues and solvents, though widely socially disapproved of, is also legal in many countries. Even so, glue and solvent use is generally considered together with illegal drug use. Tea and coffee are excluded from this review.

*Tobacco.* Most surveys of tobacco have been focused on smoking patterns within various sub-populations, on the frequency of smoking and on factors related to smoking. For that matter, the same limitations can be distinguished with regard to the survey method, as has been noted in relation to alcohol studies. The issue of under-reporting is of particular importance, and, for tobacco surveys, may be becoming an even more serious problem (Warner 1979). Several studies have examined the issue of under-reporting in tobacco surveys. Self-reported tobacco use has been checked by several methods, including biochemical measures (Haley, Axelrad and Tilton 1983, Bauman and Koch 1983, Williams and Gillies 1984).

Studies of tobacco use have relatively little relevance to concern about adverse social consequences such as those often associated with the misuse of alcohol and illegal drugs. Tobacco studies have been primarily concerned with measuring levels of use and health-related problems such as lung cancer. As noted above, surveys are not generally a good vehicle for the study of health problems, since these affect only a minority of those likely to be interviewed.

*Minor Tranquillizers and Sedatives.* A number of population surveys have been conducted which have examined the use of minor tranquillisers and sedatives. The extent of the use of such drugs can be measured by counting the number of drugs sold, the number of prescriptions for some drugs, or by counting the number of users. Each method has its own limitations.

In measuring the extent of drug use by counting the number of prescriptions it is not known how this 'potential' consumption coincides with real consumption. The same is true with regard to the counting of the number of drugs sold. Patients may not comply with medical advice. In a population survey it is possible to measure the number of users and the amount used, and a variety of factors related to the use of these drugs (Parry, Balter, Mellinker, Cisin and Manheimes 1973, Uhlenhuth, Balter and Lipman 1978). It is also possible to study the problems associated with the use of minor tranquillisers and sedatives (Curran and Golombok 1985). The use of surveys for this purpose is impeded by the types of difficulties already noted by Jasinski and Simpura in relation to alcohol related problems: (Under-reporting will occur: forgetting, intended or unintended under-reporting). On the other hand, different sorts of problems can be measured, namely, physical and psychological dependence on drugs; problems caused by side effects and by misuse of drugs (consciously or unconsciously); and social problems such as accidents (in traffic, at home, at work, etc.). An important field of study is the measurement of the prevalence of the combined use of different drugs. This topic is elaborated by Keup in Chapter 12.

*Illicit Drug Use.* 'Illicit drug use' includes the use of substances such as cannabis (marihuana, hashish), LSD, cocaine and opiates (such as heroin). Some researchers have also, for convenience, included the recreational use of glues and solvents under this heading (e.g. Plant, Peck and Samuel 1985). It is very difficult to estimate how many people use these drugs, how many are addicted and how many have (other) problems connected with the use of these substances. In the case of tobacco, alcohol and minor tranquillizers it is very useful to undertake population surveys, but such studies face more problems in relation to illicit drug use. Under-reporting will always occur with respect to the use of licit drugs, but may be much greater in relation to illicit drugtaking. Under-reporting may be considerable, because illicit drugtaking is by definition punishable by law. Surveys may only partly be useful by measuring changes in the drug use of various subpopulations, but only when it is justified to start from the principle that the amount of under-reporting will remain about the same over a period of time. Plant *et al.* (1985) have also noted some evidence of probable *over-reporting* from a study of adolescent drug use. Other methods of eliciting data about illicit drug use are also flawed. Data from health and social service agencies do not indicate the extent or nature of drug use in the community. Information from 'key informants' may also be subjective or innacurate. Such data may, however, sometimes be a better guide than surveys. Even so, drug surveys do serve a useful purpose. They have become fairly well developed, especially in North America, and provide an invaluable indication of the general, though not the precise, extent of drug use and of trends in drug use. It does seem, however, that survey research is, as yet, better developed in relation to alcohol than in relation to illegal drugs. Many methodological problems remain unsolved. As illicit drug use becomes a more pressing problem in many countries drug surveys are likely to become more commonplace and methodologies need to be improved (Rootman and Hughes 1980, Johnston 1980, Hughes, Uenufet, Khant, Medina, Mora, Navaratnam, Poshyachinda, Rootman, Salam and Wadud 1980, Smart, Hughes, Johnston, Anumonye, Khant, Medina Mora, Hanmaratnam, Poshyachinda, Varma and Wadud 1980, Smart, Arif, Hughes, Medina Mora, Navaratnam, Varma and Wadud 1981).

## Conclusions and Ideas About Future Research

The survey method is very useful in measuring the prevalence of problems related to the use of alcohol and other licit drugs, particularly substances such as minor tranquillizers and sedatives. However, the survey method has some limitations. The main flow of population surveys is the underestimation which occurs in measuring the use of alcohol and other drugs and their related problems. Population surveys are, however, much better equipped to handle some sorts of problems than others. Health problems are more difficult to measure than are social problems. With regard to alcohol problems, overall scores of 'problem drinking' have sometimes been constructed. This may be useful to get a general view of the prevalence of alcohol problems in different geographical areas or in various subpopulations. Even so, this aggregation of data often leads to failure to examine problems individually, or at least, in proper detail.

It is probable that illicit drug use is harder to examine by population surveys. Other methods may be required, such as observation studies, 'snowball surveys', key informant or multisource studies (Plant 1975, Adler 1985, Hartnoll, Daviaud, Lewis and Mitcheson 1985). The use of some drugs, such as cannabis, may be less difficult to examine by surveys if such drug use is not severely disapproved of by young people.

In view of the present state of affairs, what may be expected from future research and which topics are of importance for further study? A few general remarks can be made:
  •A growing application of all kinds of methodological 'tools' in the field of alcohol and drugs research is expected. More attention is required to questions such as: 'To what extent are results of survey-research on alcohol and drugs influenced by the presence of others during interviews?'. 'What is the role of socially desirable answering?'. 'Which methods of data

collection are preferable in which situation?'. 'Which recall period is desirable?', and so on;

• For better understanding, more comparative surveys on alcohol and drugs-related problems in different nations, and thus different cultures, are needed;

• It is also desirable to undertake more studies focused on poly drug use and related problems. The combined use of different drugs, for instance, alcohol and tranquillizers, or tranquillizers and drugs such as heroin and cocaine, has its own problems. Furthermore, the clustering of more risky habits is important, for example, drinking alcohol, smoking, taking pills and malnutrition. Are there certain 'high risk groups' to distinguish?

• Following the latter point, it seems useful to study both interrelations between alcohol and drug related problems and other variables such as all kinds of demographic, health and lifestyle variables. In this respect it is desirable to add more questions about alcohol and drugs to general health surveys;

• Last, but not least, it is necessary for alcohol and drug researchers to pay more attention to the translation of the results of their studies into recommendations useful for policymakers and/or workers in the health and social services.

REFERENCES

Adler, P. (1985) *Wheeling and Dealing: An Ethnography of an Upper-Level Drug Dealing and Smuggling Community*, New York: Columbia University Press.

Bauman, K.E. and Koch, G.G. (1983) Validity of self-reports and descriptive and analytical conclusions: the case of cigarette smoking by adolescents and their mothers, *American Journal of Epidemiology* 118, 90–8.

Cahalan, D. (1976) *Problem Drinkers*, San Francisco: Jossey-Bass.

Curran, V. and Golombok, S. (1985) *Bottling It Up*, London: Faber and Faber.

Garretsen, H.F.L. (1983) *Probleemdrinken*, Lisse: Swets and Zeitlinger.

Garretsen, H.F.L. (1984) Underestimation of problem drinking through the survey method, *Medicine and Law* 3, 399–404.

Garretsen, H.F.L. (1985) Developments with regard to alcohol consumption and alcohol-related problems: A working paper, Rotterdam: Municipal Health Service, Department of Epidemiology, No. 13.

Garretsen, H.F.L. and Knibbe, R.A. (1984) Drinking problems in the Netherlands, intercorrelations and relation with consumption level. Paper presented at Alcohol Epidemiology Section, ICAA, Edinburgh, 4–8 June.

Garretsen, H.F.L. and Knibbe, R.A. (1985) Two Dutch surveys on problem drinking, *Medicine and Law* 4, 265–68.

Haley, N.J., Axelrad, C.M. and Tilton, K.A. (1983) Validation of self-reported smoking behaviour: Biochemical analysis of cotinine and thiocyanate, *American Journal of Public Health* 73, 1204–7.

Hartnoll, R., Daviaud, I., Lewis, R. and Mitcheson, M. (1985) *Drug Problems: Assessing Local Need (A Practical Manual for Assessing the Nature and Extent of Problematic Drug Use in a Community)*, London: Drug Indicators Project.

Hughes, P.H., Venulet, J., Khant, U., Medina-Mora, M.E., Navaratnam, V. Poshyachinda, V., Rootman, I., Salam, R. and Wadud, K.A. (1980) *Core Data For Epidemiological Studies and Nonmedical Drug Use.* WHO Offset Publication No. 56, Geneva: WHO.

Jellinek, E.M. (1960) *The Disease Concept of Alcoholism*, Newhaven, Conn.: Hillhouse.

Johnston, L. (1980) *Review of General Population Surveys of Drug Use.* WHO Offset Publication No. 92, Geneva: WHO.

Knibbe, R.A., Drop, M.J., Reek, J. van and Saenger, G. (1985) The developments of alcohol consumption in the Netherlands: 1958–1981, *British Journal of Addiction* 80, 411–19.

Ledermann, S. (1956) *Alcool, Alcoolisme, Alcoolisation: Données Scientifiques de Caratere Physiologique, Economique et Social*, Institut National d'Etudes Demographiques, Travaux et Documents, Cahier No. 29, Paris, Press Universitaires de France.

Leonard, L., Dunn, N.J. and Jacob, T. (1983) Drinking problems of alcoholics: correspondence between self and spouse reports, *Addictive Behaviours* 8, 369–73.

Mulder, P.G.H. and Garretsen, H.F.L. (1983) Are epidemiological and sociological surveys a proper instrument for detecting true problem drinkers?, *International Journal of Epidemiology* 12, 442–44.

Mulford, H.A. and Wilson, R.W. (1966) *Identifying Problem Drinkers in a Household Health Survey*, Washington: National Centre for Health Statistics, Series 2, 16.

Parry, H.J., Balter, M.B., Mellinker, G.D., Cisin, I.H. and Manheimes, D.I. (1973) National patterns of psychotherapeutic drug use, *Archives of General Psychiatry* 28, 769–83.

Pernanen, K. (1974) Validity of survey data on alcohol use. In Gibbins, R.J. *et al. Research advantage in alcohol and drug problems*, vol. 1, New York: Wiley.

Peters, H.J. (1982) *Typologie Alcoholverslaafden I.*, Amsterdam: Jellinekcentrum.

Philipsen, H., Knibbe, R.A. and Reek, J. van (1983) Alcohol consumption in the Netherlands as a social phenomenon. In *Alcohol, Health and Society*, proceedings of a symposium, Zeist: TNO.

Plant, M.A. (1975) *Drugtakers in an English Town*, London: Tavistock.

Plant, M.A., Peck, D.F. and Samuel, E. (1985) *Alcohol, Drugs and School-Leavers*, London: Tavistock.

Poikolainan, K. and Karkainen, P. (1983) Diary gives more accurate information about alcohol consumption than questions, *Drug and Alcohol Dependence* 11, 209–16.

Room, R. (1977) Measurement and distribution of drinking patterns and problems in general populations. In Edwards, G., Gross, M.M., Keller, M., Moser, J. and Room, R. (eds) *Alcohol-Related Disabilities*, WHO Offset Publication No. 32, pp. 61–88, Geneva: WHO.

Rootman, I. and Hughes, P.H. (1980) *Drug-Abuse Reporting Systems*, WHO Offset Publication No. 55, Geneva: WHO.

Smart, R.G., Arif, A., Hughes, P., Medina-Mora, H.E., Navaratnam, V., Varma, V.K. and Wadud, K.A. (1981) *Drug Use Among Non-Student*

*Youth*, WHO Offset Publication No. 6, Geneva: WHO.

Smart, R.G., Hughes, P.H., Johnston, L.D., Anumonye, A., Khant, V., Medina-Mora, M.A., Hanmaratnam, V., Poshyachinda, V., Varma, V.E. and Wadud, K.A. (1980) *A Methodology for Student Drug Use Surveys*, WHO Offset Publication No. 50, Geneva: WHO.

Uhlenhuth, E.H., Balter, M.B. and Lipman, R.S. (1978) Minor tranquillizers, *Archives of General Psychiatry* 35, 650–55.

Vaillant, G.E., Gale, L. and Milofsky, E.S. (1982) Natural history of male alcoholism II, *Journal of Studies on Alcohol*, 43, 216–32.

Walsh, B.M. and Walsh, D. (1973) Validity of indices of alcoholism, *British Journal of Preventive Social Medicine* 27, 18–26.

Warner, K.E. (1979) Clearing the air waves: The cigarette and bar revisited, *Policy Analysis* 5, 4, 435–450.

Williams, R. and Gillies, P., (1984) Do we need objective measures to validate self-reported smoking?, *Public Health* 98, 294–98.

# 8. How to Measure Alcohol-related problems Amongst Young People in Community Surveys

SALME AHLSTRÖM

*Abstract*. In the early 1970s many countries began to use surveys to collect data which would either support or refute alarming reports of the prevalence of young people's drinking. Such surveys fall into two main categories. The first may be designated as exclusively descriptive, or as exploratory. The second category have either had a theoretical basis or employed more rigorous sampling procedures. The majority of surveys have had cross-sectional designs. The samples used in national surveys differ in relation to age groups and representativeness. Surveys have collected a wide range of data on young people's drinking. A few studies have included questions about whether young people have been involved in difficulties with their families, friends, or officialdom because of drinking, and some have investigated the prevalence of drunken driving and accidents caused by drinking.

The main problem in using survey techniques is that the incidence of alcohol misuse may be low. The survey method is probably better suited to examining young people's drinking patterns than to examining the consequences of their drinking.

## Introduction

Young people are an important subgroup. Adolescence is a period when social norms and values are simultaneously adopted and criticized. In many countries, adolescence is a culturally defined time of emancipation and maturation.

Society at large tends to pay a great deal of attention to the way young people drink. Part of this concern reflects a genuine worry about the future of the next generation. Nevertheless, some societies have allowed their anxiety about young people's drinking to blind them to the serious effects caused by adult drinking, the use

71

of tobacco, prescribed and illegal drugs as well as other social problems.

The consumption of alcohol has risen in both industrialized and in many developing countries since World War II. In some countries, opinions about young people's drinking and its associated problems have conflicted with each other or have been exaggerated.

During the early 1970s the harm caused by young people's drinking provoked an upsurge of concern. The survey method was widely employed to collect data which would either support or refute reports of the prevalence of young people's drinking (e.g. Davies and Stacey 1972, Ahlström-Laakso 1975, Smart 1976, O'Connor 1978, and Muller 1979). During the past twenty years a considerable body of information about this topic has been accumulated.

### THE SURVEY METHOD

The survey is an all-round tool for filling data matrices. Few people would dispute how important the survey method is and the part it has played in furthering sociology. It has proved indispensable for clarifying the human condition and providing insights into social theory. The rapid development of social science of the last few decades might not have taken place without it. The very success of the survey method, however, now also warrants an assessment of its scope and limitations (Galtung 1967). The survey method was – and is – merely one of the tools which social science employs to bring its research targets into sharper focus.

When researchers became interested in young people's drinking in the 1950s, the survey was a popular choice of research method. It was relatively easy to reach young people through the educational system or to take representative samples in geographically defined urban settings. The studies of the 1950s and 1960s were inspired by theoretical ideas (e.g. Strauss and Bacon 1953, Jessor, Graves, Hanson and Jessor 1968) or by a certain degree of liberal attitudes to alcohol policy (Bruun and Hauge 1963).

Broadly speaking, such surveys fall into two main categories. The first group may be designated as exclusively descriptive, and has frequently been purely exploratory. These surveys were often conducted within tightly fixed geographical limits, or used samples which represented only one atypical subgroup of young people, such as those in certain classes at school. Such studies did not avail themselves of the experiences of established research centres and neither were they part of a wider programme of research. The second category, however, had a more ambitious point of departure. They either had a theoretical basis or else employed representative samples in order that their findings might have more general relevance. Indeed, some of them did both.

## Study Design

The majority of surveys which focused on young people's drinking or the problems it causes have had cross-sectional study designs. Some, however, collected retrospective data, asking questions about how old respondents had been when they first began to drink and experiment with various categories of alcoholic beverage. Research in North America and in the Nordic countries in particular, has sought to monitor temporal trends in alcohol use by collecting data at fixed intervals with cross-sectional studies which employ comparable samples (e.g. Irgens-Jensen and Rud 1978, Ahlström 1979, Smart and Fejer 1975 and Rachal, Maisto, Guess and Hubbard 1980).

Longitudinal studies are much fewer. Some of them have had theoretical points of departure and have been conducted in a technically sophisticated way (Fillmore 1974, Donovan, Jessor and Jessor 1983, and Pulkkinen 1983). The time span involved has varied from a very brief one to three years, to much longer periods. The more prolonged studies have set out to clarify how well the drinking of the young person can be used to predict the drinking habits of the adult. They have not, in other words, been concerned with the evolution of young people's drinking in itself.

## Samples

The samples used in national surveys differ from each other in two respects: Firstly, in relation to target age groups and, secondly, according to how representative they have been. The age groups selected reflect the biological and social maturity of young people at the time the study is carried out. The youngest age group which the studies of the 1960s included was usually 14-year-olds; US studies dealing with the incidence of alcohol use of children aged 12 and under, for instance, were rare before 1970. Currently young people reach biological maturity earlier than was the case twenty years ago, and the youngest survey study group is now often 12-year-olds. Nevertheless, it should be noted that the biological changes accompanying puberty which usually mark the onset of adolescence vary according to environmental factors – for example, nutrition and geographical location. Better nutrition has been the most obvious reason for the secular growth trends in the height development and in the maturation process. Increasing migration has decreased the effects of genetic factors (van Wieringen 1978).

The biological changes accompanying puberty can be measured and observed. Adolescence itself, however, cannot be so easily defined. The common view is that adolescence is over when the individual becomes fully initiated into adult roles and responsibilities. But the adoption of adult roles becomes increasingly delayed as cultures become more and more complex. In the developing countries, and where social deprivation prevails, adolescence may be very brief indeed. In the industrialized countries, on the other hand, adolescence tends to last for much longer. Furthermore, young people in many countries now spend longer at school and find it harder to embark on their adult careers, with the result that the onset of adulthood is turning into a new social interlude or overlap between childhood and maturity.

The representativeness of samples used in national surveys also varies between geographical settings. Most studies have employed samples drawn from the capital city of the country in question or have concentrated on selected towns or provinces. It is relatively unusual for samples to be representative of young people as a whole. Frequently, for instance, the educational system is used to select the groups to be studied; secondary (high school) students are the most common subjects.

## Data Collection Methods

Methodological reference works for social research abound with both general and detailed advice on how to conduct interviews. Interviewing is considered to be a better way of collecting data than is the use of questionnaires. Use of the latter is often prompted by the fact that they are cheaper than interviews.

Nevertheless, the antithesis between interviews on the one hand and questionnaires on the other is largely artificial. The question of which data collection method is the better one quite simply cannot be answered. Neither, furthermore, should one forget the fact that data collection is a process of interaction, no matter whether it takes place orally or by writing.

Interviews and questionnaires can be used to complement each other. On the one hand, interview data can be amplified at a later date through questionnaires. Alternatively, questionnaires can be used to delimit the target group for subsequent detailed interviews. It is also possible to use hybrid forms which are a mixture of interview and questionnaire.

When young people are being interviewed, the age of the interviewer should be taken into consideration – especially if 'difficult' subjects such as love, sex, and drinking are involved. Questionnaires are also more reliable than interviews in relation to such matters; the more socially condemned a given form of behaviour is, the more unreliable the answers given to interview questions about it will be. People are more likely to admit blackouts and drinking to help them recover from a hangover in self completed questionnaires than in verbal interviews (Björkman 1971).

The data collection methods used in surveys of young people's drinking have, in effect, often been selected because youngsters can easily be reached through the school system. Different countries, however, have varied traditions of collecting data for alcohol research. For example, in the USA surveys have often been conducted by telephone interviews, in Norway and Sweden by questionnaires and in Finland by both interviews and questionnaires.

### TOPICS FOR CONSIDERATION

National surveys of young people's alcohol consumption and alcohol-related consequences differ widely according to the particular problem being examined and the variables being used to examine it. More detailed surveys collect a very wide range of data on both young people's drinking, alcohol-related problems, and also on the aspects of their lives and social backgrounds which are linked to alcohol use. More specific surveys, however, restrict themselves to examining alcohol use with reference to a few variables, and may ignore social factors altogether.

Questions aimed at elucidating background factors, on the other hand, have centred on the young people's surroundings (geographical location, type of housing area), the conditions in which respondents live (parents' social status, income level, available spending money), respondent's career (whether at school or working), social relationships (dating, gang membership), and on hobbies and pastimes.

The aspects which surveys of young people's drinking have focused on include, for example, the age at which a young person first had an alcoholic drink, how much he or she consumed on each drinking occasion, drinking frequency, how much he or she drank within a given period (fortnight/month/year), and drinking contexts. These factors are sometimes examined in great detail.

Popular methods of conceptualizing young people's involvement with alcohol have been: (1) To identify young people who have entered an alcoholism treatment facility; (2) To apply the adult diagnostic criteria of the alcohol dependence syndrome; (3) To apply psychological measures related to the alcohol dependence syndrome in adults to adolescents.

The first method of definition has inherent self-selecting qualities that can cause difficulties when attempting to identify the scope of this problem. Probably the most striking flaw of the two other methods is that these instruments were standardized on adult subjects. In consequence, they have no empirical validity in relation to adolescents. Some of the items on these instruments are not obviously relevant to young people. Only rarely are cases of alcohol-related disease – the classic symptoms of alcohol dependence – or the adverse consequences which befall adult alcohol dependents found amongst young people (Vingilis and Smart 1981).

Even when there are physiological consequences, young people only rarely exhibit physical dependence on alcohol. The results of longitudinal research indicate that most young problem drinkers, moreover, apparently find a way out of their difficulties by their middle or late twenties (Fillmore 1974, Donovan *et al.* 1983, Pulkkinen 1983). Adolescents who drink very heavily are more likely to use illicit drugs when they become older (Kandel 1978, Plant, Peck and Samuel 1985).

However, Mayer and Filstead (1980) have designed an instrument, the Adolescent Alcohol Involvement Scale (AAIS) for identifying those teenagers who are misusing alcohol. The AAIS does not have practical applications since it was primarily designed as a research tool to facilitate the definition of alcohol misuse among young people, and it has not been applied in studies outside North America. Responses to questions included in the AAIS do not represent continuous data, and the instrument might work in a very different way depending on the sociocultural context in which it is used.

There is, however, another approach; instead of focusing on individual problem drinkers, studies can concentrate on the individual consequences of problem drinking. This approach asks questions about whether young people have been involved in difficulties with their families, friends or officialdom because of drinking (Plant, Peck and Stuart 1982, Ahlström 1984), and enquires about the prevalence of drunken driving and accidents caused by drinking, such as falls, exposure, fires, losing property, and so on (e.g. Plant, Peck and Stuart 1982). This enables the researcher to complement the picture given by official records, which only lay bare a fraction of the harm wrought by excessive alcohol use.

One important difficulty is attributable to the fact that both drinking and alcohol-related consequences often vary considerably during the lifetime of an individual. Most survey studies, however, tend to chart the consequences of drinking on a lifetime basis, partly because of the rarity of severe consequences, and perhaps, partly due to the traditional conceptualization of 'alcoholism' as a progressive disease and of drinking problems as conditions rather than events (Mäkelä 1978).

Cahalan and Room (1974) have made a very careful distinction between *current* and *lifetime* problems. They have shown, that roughly twice as many people as report current consequences of a certain kind, will report having ever had consequences of the same type. As a result, if problems are measured on a lifetime basis, it remains unknown whether they are due to current drinking patterns or belong to some earlier period in the life of the respondent.

To compare the probabilities of various consequences at different consumption levels from one study to another, one would need a common measure for reporting the consumption. According to Mäkelä (1978) annual consumption or consumption over some period of time of 100 per cent alcohol is the most obvious candidate, but only few social investigators report data in these terms.

A major advance in understanding alcohol abuse, especially in adolescence, but also in young adulthood, has come from research showing a link between problem drinking and other problematic or 'deviant' behaviour. It is increasingly clear that alcohol abuse is not isolated, but is often associated with other problem behaviours such as cigarette smoking, illicit drug use, delinquency and precocious sexual experience in youth.

## The Limitations of Surveys

There would seem to be two reasons why the survey method has been so successful. Firstly, it generates theoretically relevant data, and secondly, the resulting data can be subjected to statistical analysis (Galtung 1967). Whilst social science has never been short of relevant data, only seldom can statistical techniques be applied to them.

Of course, every research method has its limitations. Some of the survey method's flaws are very general, as already noted by Jasinski and Simpura. Problems or limitations can be due to non-contacts or refusals leading to over- or under-reporting. Others, however, are tied to the hazards of 'exporting' sociology or research methods from the industrialized countries to non-industrial or developing areas of the world.

Empirical sociology has its strongest foothold in the North Atlantic community. The survey method best lends itself to settled societies in which there is a slow rate of change and little internal conflict, and which are highly individual-oriented, inner-directed and have a high degree of correspondence between thought, word and deed (Galtung 1967). In consequence the application of survey techniques to many of the developing countries may be difficult.

One problem in using survey techniques to investigate young people's problem drinking is that the incidence of alcohol-related problems may be low. But, on the other hand, the frequency of times drunk, for instance, can be used as a 'marker variable' for targeting those young people who are likely to experience alcohol-related problems. It may well be that the survey method is better suited to analysing young people's drinking patterns than to the analysis of the consequences of problem drinking in their own right. Other methods of data collection such as observation, or documentary evidence, could be used to supplement surveys in order to obtain a more comprehensive picture of alcohol-related problems amongst young people.

### RECOMMENDATIONS

1. Longitudinal studies which set out to understand the development of drinking habits during adolescence should ideally last for 8–10 years.

2. It is very important to appreciate that cross-cultural studies need more than questionnaire forms which are just translated from one language to another. They should be founded on an overall picture of the entire culture. Consequently, each country should have a representative of its own when plans are made.

3. Representative samples of the young population as a whole are not always accessible. When they cannot be used, the research team should assess the need for additional samples. The study groups involved should not only include youngsters at school. They should also include young people who have jobs or who are unemployed, and those in important institutions such as penal establishments, rehabilitation centres, borstals, and so on.

4. The selection of target age groups is especially important since biological maturation varies from one culture to another.

5. Interviews and self-completed questionnaires should be used together, especially in developing countries. Respondents might be given verbal advice on how to complete a questionnaire, even though the replies to such an instrument are to be written down. Some respondents, especially in developing countries, are likely to be illiterate. Similarly, the completed questionnaires could be collected by the researchers themselves instead of by mail. This makes it possible to check that all the questions have been answered and understood correctly.

6. The survey method should be complemented by other approaches. Officially recorded statistical material could be employed and observational research could be considered.

7. The questionnaire/interview should include questions which would make it possible to calculate annual consumption during several time spans. This would enable the research team to assess the probability of various alcohol problems at different consumption levels.

8. Overall alcohol consumption should be complemented with quantitative measures of drinking habits, such as the frequency of drunkenness. Qualitative typologies would not be adequate in this regard.

9. Drinking and alcohol problems fluctuate over the lifetime of an individual, especially during adolescence. There should therefore be a clear distinction between questions which refer to lifetime problems and those experienced only briefly or during a short period of time.

The main problem in using survey techniques to study young people's alcohol-related problems is that the incidence of the harm associated with excessive drinking may well be low. The survey method, perhaps, is better suited to examining drinking patterns than it is to examining the consequences of problem drinking. Research is needed into how youngsters behave when drunk in order to guide social policies to curb alcohol misuse. More information is also needed about the part played by society and culture at large, its norms and social sanctions.

REFERENCES

Ahlström, S. (1979) *Trends in Drinking Habits Among Finnish Youth from the Beginning of the 1960s to the Late 1970s*, Helsinki: Reports from the Social Research Institute of Alcohol Studies No. 128.

Ahlström, S. (1984) *The Social Control of Teenage Drinking in Finland.* Paper presented at the Alcohol Epidemiology Section Meetings, ICAA, Edinburgh, June 4–8.

Ahlström-Laakso, S. (1975) *Changing Drinking Habits Among Finnish Youth*, Helsinki: Reports from the Social Research Institute of Alcohol Studies No. 81.

Björkman, N.-M. (1971) An jämförelse mellan enkät- och intervjumetodik vid insamling av data om akoholburk, *Statens offentliga utredningar*, Stockholm, 77.

Bruun, K. and Hauge, R. (1983) *Drinking Habits among Northern Youth: A Cross-National Study of Male Teenage Drinking in the Northern Capitals*, Helsinki: The Finnish Foundation for Alcohol Studies.

Cahalan, D. and Room, R. (1974) *Problem Drinking Among American Men*, New Haven, Conn.: Rutgers Center of Alcohol Studies.

Davies, J. and Stacey, B. (1972) *Teenagers and Alcohol*, London: HMSO.

Donovan, J.E., Jessor, R. and Jessor, S.L. (1983) Problem drinking in adolescence and young adulthood: A follow-up study, *Journal of Studies on Alcohol* 41, 100–37.

Fillmore, K.M. (1974) Drinking and problem drinking in early adulthood and middle age, *Quarterly Journal of Studies on Alcohol* 35, 891–40.

Galtung, J. (1967) *Theory and Methods of Social Research*, London: Allen and Unwin.

Irgens-Jensen, O. and Rud, M.G. (1978) *Bruk av stoffer, alkohol og tobakk blant ungdom i Oslo 1968–1978*, Oslo: Statens Institutt for alkoholforskning stensilserie No. 18.

Jessor, R., Graves, T.D., Hanson, R.C. and Jessor, S.O. (1968) *Society, Personality, and Deviant Behaviour: A Study of a Tri-Ethnic Community*, New York: Holt, Rinehart and Winston.

Kandel, D.B. (ed)(1978) *Longitudinal Research on Drug Use*, New York: Halstead.

Mäkelä, K. (1978) Level of consumption and social consequences of drinking. In Israel, Y., Glaser, F.B., Kalant, H., Popham, R.E., Schmidt, W. and Smart, R.G. (eds) *Research Advances in Alcohol and Drug Problems*, vol. 4, pp. 303–48, New York: Plenum.

Mayer, J.E. and Filstead, W.J. (1980) Empirical procedures for defining adolescent alcohol misuse. In Mayer, J.E. and Filstead, W.3. (eds) *Adolescence and Alcohol*, Cambridge, Mass.: Ballinger.

Müller, R. (1979) Gesamtschweizerische Repräsentativerhebung über den Alkohol und Tabakkonsum von Schulern des 6., 7. und 8. Schuljahres, *Drogalkohol* 1, 3–22.

O'Connor, J. (1978) *The Young Drinkers*, London: Tavistock.

Plant, M.A., Peck, D.F. and Samuel, F. (1985) *Alcohol, Drugs and School-Leavers*, London: Tavistock.

Plant, M.A., Peck, D.F. and Stuart, R. (1982) Self-reported drinking habits and alcohol-related consequences amongst a cohort of Scottish teenagers, *British Journal of Addiction* 77, 75–90.

Pulkkinen, L. (1983) Youthful smoking and drinking in a longitudinal perspective, *Journal of Youth and Adolescence* 12, 253–83.

Rachal, J.V., Maisto, S.A., Guess, L.L. and Hubbard, R.L. (1980) *A National Study of Adolescent Drinking Behavior – 1978*. Final report prepared for the National Institute on Alcohol Abuse and Alcoholism under Contract No. ADM-281-76-0019, N.C., Research Triangle Institute, Research Traingle Park.

Smart, R. (1976) *New Drinkers, Teenage Use and Abuse of Alcohol*, Toronto, Ontario: Addiction Research Foundation.

Smart, R.G. and Fejer, D. (1975) Six years of cross-sectional surveys of student drug use in Toronto, *Bulletin on Narcotics* 27, 11–22.

Strauss, R. and Bacon, S.D. (1953) *Drinking in College*, New Haven, Conn.: Yales University Press.

van Wieringen, J.C. (1978) Secular growth changes. In Falkner, F. and Tanner, J.M. (eds) *Human Growth 2, Postnatal Growth*, pp. 445–73. New York: Plenum.

Vingilis, E. and Smart, R.G. (1981) Physical dependence on alcohol in youth. In Israel, Y., Glaser, F.B., Kalant, H., Popham, R.E., Schmidt, W. and Smart, R.G. (eds) *Research Advances in Alcohol and Drug Problems*, vol. 6, pp. 197–215. New York, Plenum.

# 9. The Relationship Between Alcohol Consumption Patterns and the Harmful Consequences of Drinking

ESA ÖSTERBERG

*Abstract*. This chapter brings together the results of a number of studies of the relationship between alcohol use and the harmful effects of drinking. It describes how this association has been approached, some research findings and the kind of problems these involve. A discussion is also presented of what information is needed on the relationship between alcohol consumption, drinking habits and alcohol-related problems.

Many studies have shown that *per capita* alcohol consumption is an accurate indicator of the problems related to prolonged heavy alcohol use, such as liver cirrhosis mortality. Changes in total alcohol consumption are also often related to trends in the social consequences of drinking.

One promising way of increasing knowledge of the relationship between drinking and alcohol-related problems is through detailed surveys. Information about the annual consumption of pure alcohol needs to be reinforced by indicators of drinking style. Measures used to describe alcohol-related consequences also need more standardizing.

General population surveys are cumbersome tools and not well suited to describing temporal changes in the levels of adverse alcohol-related consequences. Time series analysis provides a promising approach to the examination of such trends.

## Introduction

It is widely recognized that drinking alcohol causes problems in every society. Such problems may be classified according to whether they mainly affect public health, or are social and economic. These categories frequently overlap. It is often difficult to judge whether the 'cause' of an alcohol-related consequence was acute intoxication or continuous heavy drinking. Nevertheless, it often makes sense to try to distinguish between the effects of long-term heavy consumption and the results of single drinking occasions. This is true from both social and health perspectives.

Discussion of the relationship between alcohol consumption and the consequences of drinking has chiefly focused on continuous heavy drinking and its impact on health. It is often presupposed that there is strong positive association between average alcohol consumption and a number of alcohol-related ailments. The social and economic problems caused by drinking, on the other hand, are viewed as being more related to certain qualitative patterns of alcohol use than to the quantities of liquor consumed in themselves. Indeed, alcohol-related social problems are often thought to vary independently of – sometimes even inversely with – the amount of alcohol consumed.

This chapter brings together the results of a number of studies pertaining to the relationship between alcohol consumption patterns and the harmful consequences of drinking. It describes how the relationship has been approached, highlights some key findings and the kind of problems these studies involved. Suggestions are presented about what information is needed on the relationship between alcohol consumption, drinking patterns and alcohol-related problems.

## ADVERSE CONSEQUENCES TO HEALTH

Evidence related to the adverse consequences of heavy drinking on physical health mainly stems from five fields of research: the drinking histories of persons suffering from a particular disease or trauma; the prevalence of physical health problems in samples of heavy drinkers; the mortality of heavy drinkers; the drinking history of persons who die from a specific cause; and regional and temporal variations in cause-specific death rates related to indices of the prevalence of heavy drinking. Taken as a whole, morbidity studies present a reasonably consistent picture of the physical health problems likely to be found among heavy drinkers. These include diseases of the nervous system, such as peripheral neuropathy, and various indicators of brain damage; diseases of the digestive system, especially ailments of the liver, acute and chronic gastritis, peptic ulcers and pancreatitis; respiratory diseases, particularly chronic bronchitis, pneumonia and tuberculosis; cardiovascular diseases, especially cardiomyopathy and hypertension; certain cancers – those of the upper respiratory and upper digestive tracts in particular; and injuries resulting from road traffic and other accidents (Bruun, Edwards, Lumio, Mäkelä, Pan, Popham, Room Schmidt, Skog, Sulkunen and Österberg (1975).

As might be expected in view of the morbidity data, mortality studies consistently reveal significantly elevated death rates in samples of alcoholics and other heavy drinkers. It can, therefore, be concluded that heavy users of alcohol – whether identified in clinical situations, through case-finding surveys, on the basis of records of arrests for drunkenness, or through reported drinking habits – have a substantially elevated risk of premature death. Yet the mortality rate may vary substantially, depending on how users are identified. It should also be noted that not all of the alcohol-related causes of death are necessarily associated with long-term rather than short-term heavy consumption. In particular, it is clear that deaths from accidents are often associated with specific episodes of intoxication irrespective of chronicity.

An important question posed by the occurrence of a higher death rate among heavy drinkers is the relative causal role of alcohol consumption and factors associated with heavy drinking, such as heavy smoking, illegal drug use, emotional problems and personal neglect. Heavy drinkers, for instance, are often heavy smokers, and the excess mortality in lung cancer among heavy drinkers has in fact been explained with references to smoking. The findings of Bruun *et al.* (1975) in this respect were three-fold. Firstly, the effects of alcohol explain a considerable part of the excess mortality of heavy drinkers. Secondly, the aetiological importance of alcohol is clear with respect to deaths from liver cirrhosis, accidents, and cancers of the upper digestive and upper respiratory tracts, and unclear with respect to most cardiovascular diseases. Thirdly, other factors often associated with heavy drinking are probably largely or entirely responsible for the elevated death rates from tuberculosis, lung cancer and suicide.

These conclusions lead to a question which, if answered in the affirmative, is of great practical importance: Is there a certain level of alcohol consumption which clearly increases the general mortality rate, and is there a boundary between 'safe' and 'hazardous' alcohol consumption levels? It seems, however, that the lowest level of chronic alcohol consumption which constitutes a significant hazard to longevity has yet to be determined. A similar lack of basic information exists in relation to the health effects of prescribed and illegal drugs.

84

The prevalence of heavy alcohol consumption, irrespective of how this is defined, is likely to rise and fall with the average consumption of the population. Variation in *per capita* consumption – either from one region to another or over time in the same region – should therefore be accompanied by similar variations in the health damage resulting from heavy drinking. With respect to liver cirrhosis, the results of cross-sectional and time series analyses confirm what mortality and morbidity studies would lead one to expect: The rate of death from liver cirrhosis usually rises and falls with the level of alcohol consumption in the general population. There are also indications of the expected relationship with regard to oesophageal cancer, but the overall picture is unclear.

The co-variation of *per capita* alcohol consumption and indices of damage to health is not always easy to detect. The available measurements are often subject to sources of considerable variation which can obscure any effect of changes in consumption levels. Nevertheless, the alcohol consumption level is, in most cases, a highly accurate predictor of the cirrhosis death rate. There is also suggestive evidence, noted in several temporal series, of co-variation between consumption and general mortality when the latter is understood as the excess of male over female mortality in the middle age range (Bruun *et al.* 1975).

## ADVERSE SOCIAL CONSEQUENCES

Numerous studies show that drinking is associated with a wide array of social consequences – violent crimes, employment problems, family problems, financial difficulties and so on. But if one wishes to ask more detailed questions about the relationship between alcohol consumption and the social problems associated with drinking – the relative impact of the amount and pattern of alcohol intake, the social position of the drinker, and how the environment controls different types of consequences, for example – one has to refer to fragmentary evidence. The majority of general population studies dealing with the consequences of drinking seem to aim at determining the prevalence of problem drinkers. Relatively little has been done to show how actual consumption level and drinking patterns interact with environmental reactions to produce alcohol problems (Mäkelä 1978, Collins 1982).

There are several approaches to the relationship between drinking and its numerous social consequences. Firstly, there are studies in which the sample scrutinized is defined by some event or consequence related to alcohol. The drinking characteristics of the sample are then analysed with the aim of determining the proportion of heavy drinkers, how many people meet a given clinical criterion of 'dependence', or simply how many people have an elevated blood alcohol level. Another type of study presents data on the incidence of different alcohol-related problems among known heavy drinkers or 'alcoholics'. Thirdly, there are investigations which present individual data on drinking and alcohol-related consequences among both clinical and general population samples. Fourthly, there are cross-regional and temporal studies of the relationship between drinking and its social consequences.

Turning to individuals, there seems to be a positive relationship between overall alcohol intake and the adverse consequences of drinking (Mäkelä 1978). Most of the injurious social consequences of drinking, however, are probably more closely related to a given pattern of drinking rather than to total alcohol consumption. Furthermore, much of the variation in consequences remains unexplained even when there is detailed information about the frequency of drinking and the quantities consumed.

When they reach a given level of consumption, young people tend to run into severe trouble. This is presumably due to their drinking habits and the fact that inexperienced drinkers react more visibly than do regular drinkers to the same amount of alcohol. At the other end of the scale, the tolerance of chronically alcohol dependent individuals tends to decrease again. There are also gender differences in the social consequences of drinking. The bulk of this discrepancy is obviously explained by the fact that women tend to drink much less than men in most countries. It is, however, possible that, if the overall amount of intake and frequency of drunkenness were constant the social consequences of drinking amongst men and women would still fluctuate because of gender-based differences in both behaviour and social control. Finally, social control influences the pattern of associations between alcohol consumption levels, patterns of drinking and the social consequences of alcohol consumption.

Both researchers and policy-makers clearly need more detailed knowledge of the hazardous levels of alcohol (and drug) consumption from the point of view of various health problems. With the exception of the risk of accidents – traffic accidents in particular – corresponding data for the social consequences of drinking would be less obviously useful.

The general impression obtained from literature on the subject is that the first signs of adverse social reactions appear at relatively low levels of drinking. At the other extreme, some individuals seem to be able to drink heavily for long periods without apparently encountering social problems. Most societies have made drunken driving a crime as a result of an extensive body of research evidence and other considerations. The proscribed blood alcohol level varies from country to country and does not necessarily coincide with the elevated risks of driving while intoxicated. The actual level – usually lying between 0.5 and 1.0 parts per thousand – is, however, of great practical significance, since arrests and convictions for drunken driving are important amongst the social consequences of drinking (Mäkelä, Room, Single, Sulkunen, Walsh, Bunce, Cahannes, Cameron, Giesbrecht, de Lint, Makinen, Morgan, Mosher, Moskalewicz, Müller, Österberg, Wald and Walsh 1981, Ross 1984).

Until now, there have been few regional comparisons of the social consequences of drinking. What work has been done shows virtually no conclusive regional relationship between average consumption levels and the various social consequences of drinking (Bunce and Room 1977). This finding, as noted in Chapter 5, is probably partly due to the difficulty of obtaining comparable data together with the problems encountered in planning research projects.

Few temporal analyses of consumption levels, drinking patterns and consequences of drinking have been compiled (Giesbrecht, Cahannes, Moskalewicz, Österberg and Room 1983). The general conclusion to be drawn from such analysis is that changes in the total consumption of alcohol and drinking patterns are reflected in a range of harmful consequences of drinking. It should also be noted that cultural variations in drinking patterns are usually based on lasting historical traditions which are quite resistant to change. The social consequences of drinking are therefore sometimes related to average consumption levels in temporal analyses and to drinking patterns in cross-sectional analyses.

## TWO RECENT EXAMPLES

The data for the Scandinavian Drinking Survey were collected in 1979 in Finland, Iceland, Norway and Sweden. This study has been cited in Chapter 4. These nations have relatively low levels of alcohol consumption compared to most other European countries. There are, however, clear differences between the four nations: in 1979 the consumption was highest in Finland (7.8 litres per adult), followed by Sweden (7.1), Norway (5.6) and Iceland (4.5).

The Scandinavian Drinking Survey questionnaire examined several types of adverse consequences of drinking (Mäkelä 1981). There were no clear connections between the distributions of the answers related to negative consequences and those related to the total level of alcohol consumption. Iceland had the lowest *per capita* consumption but was the top country in reported consequences. It seems, therefore, that it is not possible to make reliable predictions of the extent of the negative consequences of drinking on the basis of a country's total alcohol consumption. On the other hand, it has been concluded that a higher level of annual consumption of respondents in each country was associated with a higher incidence of adverse consequences (Hauge and Irgens-Jensen 1986). Consequently, at the same level of consumption, the average total of negative consequences was highest in Iceland, followed by Finland, Norway and Sweden in that order.

The Scandinavian Drinking Survey directed two sets of questions towards differences in drinking patterns (Simpura 1981). First-hand experiences of intoxication and drinking occasions involving high consumption were more common in Iceland and Finland than in Norway and Sweden. In other words, the frequency of intoxication was very important in determining the frequency of adverse consequences of alcohol use. In each country there was a clear connection between annual alcohol consumption and the number of episodes of intoxication. When the frequency of intoxication remains constant there will be only minor differences in the incidence of injurious consequences in different countries. The information gathered in the Scandinavian Drinking Survey indicates that the drinking pattern itself, more precisely whether drinking alcohol leads to intoxication or not, is decisive for the social consequences of drinking. For most consequences, drinking pattern was more significant than total alcohol consumption. But the study also showed that other factors besides consumption play a role in relation to many of the adverse consequences of drinking (Hauge and Irgens-Jensen 1986).

The International Study of Alcohol Control Experiences (ISACE) presented an analysis of the social history of the post-war alcohol experiences of seven societies, namely California, Finland, Ireland, the Netherlands, Ontario, Poland and Switzerland (Mäkelä *et al.* 1981, Single, Morgan and de Lint 1981).

ISACE was highly aware of the problems involved in comparing alcohol-related problems in several settings. Different societies, for instances, define social problems in different ways and also disagree about the extent to which these problems are related to alcohol. Furthermore, societies change over time in terms of their readiness to ascribe different social problems to drinking. Important national differences also exist in the distribution of resources among the authorities concerned with the management of alcohol-related problems. This affects when and how alcohol problems are tackled and also has an effect on statistics. Most records used as problem indicators are kept by official agencies as part of their duties. This in turn means that problem indicators also reflect changes in the activity of different authorities, or fluctuations in statistical practice (Mäkelä et al. 1981).

ISACE's principal solution to the difficulty of comparing the nature and extent of alcohol-related problems was to seek measures on two dimensions; firstly, alcohol's role in problematic events or situations, and secondly, the cultural dimension in the definition of 'problems' and their attribution to alcohol. In practice, ISACE did not have access to anything near the optimum standard of data. The available time series came from four health and social statistical systems: mortality records, hospitalization records, statistics on arrests and convictions for public drunkenness, and road accident statistics. These data reflected differing mixtures of 'objective' reality and social definition and attribution. The available measures were thus severely limited as a means of describing and comparing alcohol problems in the seven societies studied.

Post-war alcohol consumption levels rose in every society studied by ISACE. Alcohol-related problems, on the other hand, showed a more complicated pattern. Increases in alcohol consumption were accompanied by increases in the incidence of many health ailments known to be causally related to prolonged drinking. Even so, the rate of increase varied from one disease and society to another. Evidence related to the consequences of single-drinking occasions was less conclusive, but even in the societies in which conflicts related to drinking had increased in absolute terms, the rate of increase was lower than that in aggregate consumption. This can be seen as an indication of less conflict-prone patterns of drinking behaviour. Drunken driving is perhaps the only type of behaviour related to single drinking occasions which steadily gained in importance. The absolute number of alcohol-related road accidents increased in each of the societies studied, and when the overall accident rate fell, the proportion of all accidents in which alcohol played a part tended to rise.

The rate of increase of health ailments related to prolonged drinking tended to be higher than the rate of increase of conflicts related to single drinking occasions. Because of the different rate of growth of various types of drinking problems, variations between societies diminished. Nevertheless, persistent cultural differences exist. In Finland and Poland in particular, social conflicts related to drunken behaviour are still extremely important. The health consequences of single drinking occasions are similarly quite important in comparison to the health consequences of prolonged drinking (Österberg 1986).

In broad terms, the findings of ISACE may be interpreted thus: Each society has certain specific cultural circumstances and drinking habits, and the range of alcohol-related problems varies accordingly. In cross-sectional comparisons, this – coupled with differences in the management of alcohol-related problems – leads to a situation in which there are few if any positive relationships between the consumption level and the incidence of specific alcohol-related problems at a particular time. Nevertheless, considering the historical experience of each cultural setting, problems are not unrelated to temporal variations in aggregate consumption. Even in a specific setting, the relationship between the consumption level and problems is by no means simple. First of all, patterns of drinking and drunken behaviour sometimes change. Secondly, many other factors besides drinking behaviour determine the rate and seriousness of alcohol problems. Urban ecology influences the probability that public drunkenness will result in social conflicts, medical technology has an impact on the incidence of fatal delirium, and so on.

## Summary and Discussion

*Per capita* alcohol consumption is quite widely used as an indicator of the level of alcohol-related problems in different societies, and is also employed as an indicator of changes in the level of the adverse consequences of drinking. Many studies show that the alcohol consumption level is, in most cases, a highly accurate indicator of the problems related to prolonged heavy alcohol use, such as liver cirrhosis mortality. Changes in total alcohol consumption are also often related to the social consequences of drinking.

Total alcohol consumption should, however, be augmented by other indicators. One promising way of increasing knowledge of the relationship between drinking and its injurious consequences is to collect general population data. Because of the many conceptual and technical difficulties connected with the composite indices commonly used in this kind of study, one should in future try to adopt less ambiguous measures. As the Scandinavian Drinking Survey shows, data on the annual *per capita* alcohol consumption should be reinforced by indicators of the style of drinking. One such measure might be the frequency of drunkenness. There are, however, technical difficulties in measuring the latter. Blood alcohol levels, for instance, vary with body weight and the speed of drinking; changes in behaviour depend on the blood alcohol concentration, the drinker's experience, tolerance and personality, and on the society in which he or she lives. Furthermore, many of the adverse consequences of drinking, such as alcohol poisoning, occur at only very high blood alcohol levels.

The measures used to describe the injurious consequences of alcohol use need to be more highly standardized. Most studies measure them on a lifetime basis because of the infrequency of serious social consequences. This does not take into account the fact that drinking and its consequences vary markedly over individuals' lifetimes. Even more difficult problems of interpretation arise from the use of rather heterogeneous composite measures which combine items from different spheres of life.

General population surveys are cumbersome and not very well suited to describing temporal changes in harmful consequences. The ISACE provides an example of another way to monitor and compare consequences in different societies and to study the relationship between drinking patterns and the consequences of drinking. It also shows that many problems connected with the time series data gathered by different official authorities can be tackled in two ways. Firstly, it is always possible to study how such problems are defined, how the statistics are collected and how and why the activities of the authorities in question change over time. Secondly, such studies should not rely on too few indicators. On the contrary, interpretations should be based on all the available relevant indicators which give a coherent picture of the situation. It would also be important to collect data on the structure of consumption, because patterns of drinking and the dominant uses of alcohol tend to coincide with the favoured type of beverage. In wine producing countries, wine can be called a food; in the spirit producing countries alcohol is mainly used as an intoxicant; and beer drinking is traditionally connected with daily social contact. The connection between a specific type of beverage and drinking patterns, however, will not necessarily persist in a new cultural context, and changes in the structure of consumption do not form very good predictors of changes in drinking patterns. In this respect, general population surveys which ask questions about drinking occasions, and the context in which drinking occurs, can be of great assistance.

REFERENCES

Bruun, K., Edwards, G., Lumio, M., Mäkelä, K., Pan, L., Popham, R.E., Room, R., Schmidt, W., Skog, O.-J., Sulkunen, P. and Österberg, E. (1975) *Alcohol Control Policies in Public Health Perspective*. Forssa: Finnish Foundation for Alcohol Studies.

Bunce, R. and Room, R. (1977) *The Interrelations of Alcohol Problems Across Nations. Preliminary Partial Report for Alcohol and Health III*, University of California: Social Research Group, School of Public Health.

Collins, J.J. (ed.)(1982) *Drinking and Crime*, London: Tavistock.

Giesbrecht, N., Cahannes, M., Moskalewicz, J., Österberg, E. and Room, R. (eds)(1983) *Consequences of Drinking: Trends in Alcohol Problem Statistics in Seven Countries*, Toronto: Addiction Research Foundation.

Hauge, R. and Irgens-Jensen, O. (1986) The relationship between alcohol consumption, alcohol intoxication and negative consequences of drinking in four Scandinavian countries, *British Journal of Addiction* 81, 513–24.

Mäkelä, K. (1978) Level of Consumption and Social Consequences of Drinking. In Israel, Y. *et al.* (eds) *Research Advances in Alcohol and Drug Problems*, vol. 4, pp. 303–48, New York: Plenum.

Mäkelä, K. (1981) *Construction of Composite Indices of Drinking Attitudes and Personal Experiences Related to Drinking in the Scandinavian Drinking Survey*, Oslo: National Institute for Alcohol Research.

Mäkelä, K., Room, R., Single, E., Sulkunen, P., Walsh, B., Bunce, R., Cahannes, M., Cameron, T., Giesbrecht, N., de Lint, J., Mäkinen, H., Morgan, P., Mosher, J., Moskalewicz, J., Müller, R., Österberg, E., Wald, I. and Walsh, D. (1981) *Alcohol, Society and the State 1. A comparative Study of Alcohol Control*, Toronto: Addiction Research Foundation.

Österberg, E. (1986) Alcohol-Related Problems in Cross-National Perspective: The Results of the International Study of Alcohol Control Experiences. In Babor, T.F. (ed) *Alcohol and Culture. Comparative Perspectives from Europe and America*. Annals of the New York Academy of Sciences, vol. 472, pp. 10–20, New York.

Ross, H.L. (1984) *Deterring the Drunken Driver*, Lexington, Mass.: Lexington Books.

Simpura, J. (1981) *Scandinavian Drinking Survey: Construction of alcohol intake*, Oslo: National Institute for Alcohol Research.

Single, E., Morgan, P. and de Lint, J. (1981) *Alcohol, Society and the State, 2. The Social History of Control Policy in Seven Countries*, Toronto: Addiction Research Foundation.

# PART TWO

## PATTERNS OF USE AND

## POLICY IMPLICATIONS

# 10. The Use of Official Data in Measuring Patterns of Drug Use in the Community: Merits and Limitations

MARIE CHOQUET and SILVIE LEDOUX

*Abstract.* The prevention of drug misuse is likely to be assisted by research that determines the levels and patterns of drug use and misuse in the community. Such research should indicate the demographic, social and psychological characteristics of drug users and the traits of those who are most exposed to risks of adverse consequences. Such surveys generally require considerable time and funding. They also involve a variety of methodological problems. Some of these are discussed in this chapter, together with the uses of 'official data' for the measurement of different forms of drug use in the community.

## Introduction

In many countries statistics are routinely collected which provide an indirect means of examining drug use and misuse. These may be referred to as 'official data', that is, information systematically collected at regular intervals on a national or regional scale, or by local agencies and institutions. Such data are often published in the form of reports which may be more or less accessible or which may be confidential. This type of information includes:

Mortality data

Morbidity data

Prescription and retail pharmacy records

Police and court statistics

Economic statistics.

The purpose of this brief review is to give an outline of the different indirect indicators of drug use and misuse, and to critically assess their value, availability, reliability, validity and relevance. In order to illustrate the complexity of the use of such information, methodological problems involved in drug consumption survey will be briefly discussed. Some of these 'indirect indicators' may be classified 'official data' and are also discussed.

## INDIRECT APPROACHES TO ASSESSING PSYCHOACTIVE DRUG CONSUMPTION

The possible stages related to psychoactive drug consumption are indicated by the following diagram:

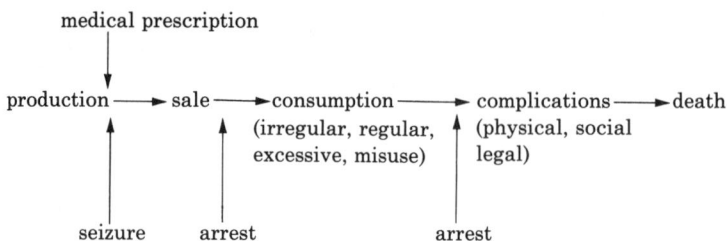

```
        medical prescription
                  |
                  v
production ──────► sale ──────► consumption ────────► complications ──────► death
            ▲           ▲       (irregular, regular,  ▲  (physical, social
            |           |        excessive, misuse)   |   legal)
            |           |                             |
          seizure     arrest                        arrest
```

According to the drug considered, the different factors in the diagram appear or do not appear (there is little evidence of legal complications arising from the use of tobacco!), are accessible or not (there are no figures available for the production and sale of illicit drugs!), essential or not (a medical prescription is not needed for tobacco or alcohol!). The analysis therefore has to be adapted in terms of these different facts, and for this reason the available data will be dealt with first, followed by their relevance to different psychoactive drugs.

As noted by Anokhina and Ivanets in Chapter 5, indicators obviously do not always have the same significance, availability or reliability in different countries or regions. In this short review it is impossible to take such variations into account, since they are difficult to identify without a wealth of cross-cultural evidence. In order to make available statistics more comparable, definitions and methods of collecting data in different countries need to be clarified, and, if possible, standardized. This is a recurring theme of this monograph. It is hoped that this chapter will serve to highlight the need for such advances.

## INDIRECT STATISTICS RELATED TO DRUG USE IN THE COMMUNITY

### Mortality Data

Mortality statistics are based on death certificates. Apart from the usual socio-demographic information (age, sex, socio-economic category), these certificates mention: the immediate cause of death, the initial cause (i.e. the nature of the disease responsible), and complementary information concerning morbidity having contributed to the fatal issue. Most countries use the ICD 9 procedure for codifying immediate and initial causes (Hartnoll, Daviaud, Lewis and Mitchison 1985, Ministère des Affaires Sociales et de la Solidarité Nationale et au Secretariat d'Etat Chargé de la Santé 1985).

Mortality data are an indication of problem drug taking, and therefore cannot be considered an indicator of consumption, in spite of the relation between 'excessive' drug use and mortality. This connection varies from one drug to another and in relation to modes and patterns of drug use (Chick 1982, Giesbrecht, Cahannes, Moskalewicz, Österberg and Room 1983, Hartnoll *et al.* 1985). Several surveys have shown that there is a relation between consumption rates, particularly for tobacco and alcohol, and drug-related death rates. In France a reduction in *per capita* alcohol consumption was followed by a fall in alcohol-related deaths.

*Availability*: In most countries mortality data are easily accessible, but statistics based on the primary and secondary causes of death are more difficult to obtain. This can lead to the underestimation of drug-related deaths. The regularity of publication for these statistics varies from one country to another, but is typically every two or three years.

*Reliability*: Although rates are probably accurate for well-defined and well-known diagnoses such as cancer and heart disease, they are less reliable for socially unacceptable 'diseases' such as overdose or alcohol dependence.

*Validity*: Mortality can be a valid indicator of excessive drug consumption or drug misuse, but does not indicate the prevalence of drug use in the community. However, significant changes in the number or the characteristics of drug-related deaths probably indicate a definite change in the extent and nature of drug use.

*Relevance*: Death rates can be taken into account in conjunction with other indicators to assess or monitor patterns of drug misuse.

*Alcohol-related deaths.* Several types of mortality are linked with excessive drinking: alcohol dependence, alcoholic poisoning, cirrhosis, alcoholic psychosis. More recently, data on cancer of the mouth, the larynx or the oesophagus are included. Sometimes suicide and traffic accidents are considered as alcohol-related deaths, but only the first group of causes can be considered reliable indicators. Many alcohol-related deaths are the result of chronic rather than acute heavy drinking (Giesbrecht *et al.* 1983, Ministère des Affaires Sociales et de la Solidarité Nationale et au Secretariat d'Etat Chargé de la Santé 1985, Got 1986). Even so, intoxication is a commonplace cause of road traffic deaths.

*Tobacco-related deaths.* Smoking may cause ischaemic heart diseases, trachea, bronchial or lung cancer and chronic obstructive lung diseases. Cancer of the bladder, lips, mouth, oesophagus and pharynx can also be related to tobacco misuse. Lung cancer is generally considered to be the best indicator (Royal College of Physicians 1983, Chandler 1986).

*Psychoactive drug-related deaths.* Suicide and accidental poisoning are often associated with excessive drug consumption, but the availability of these substances has not been established as influencing suicide rates. These statistics are probably biased by under-reporting and failure to connect many deaths with drug misuse.

*Illicit drug-related deaths.* Data concerning overdoses, suicides and accidents resulting from illicit drug use are not relevant because they tend to be unreliable. Death rates are affected by factors other than the prevalence of drug misuse, such as the doctor's awareness of the factor or the rate of drug use in the area (Hartnoll *et al.* 1985).

## Morbidity Data

*a. Hospital-based data.* Most hospitals, both public and private, publish annual statistics concerning the patients they admit, but in several countries only public hospital data are co-ordinated on a regional or national scale. The data available for each admission are: In a general hospital – the discharge diagnosis (primary or secondary diagnosis), the number of admissions (it is important to distinguish new cases from overall admissions), non-fatal drug emergency. In psychiatric hospitals: the admission diagnosis (first admission or not). These statistics are indicators of 'problematic' drug use. However, only serious physical or psychiatric complications result in hospital admission, whether for care or for treatment of dependence (Hartnoll *et al.* 1985, Ministère des Affaires Sociales et de la Solidarité Nationale au Secretariat d'Etat Chargé de la Santé 1985). Moreover, there is often a long time lapse between drug consumption and drug-related illness or contact with a treatment agency.

*Availability*: Statistics are rarely available on a national level and may sometimes only be produced by a special survey. Available data only relate to primary diagnosis and often take a long time to be published.

*Reliability*: Hospital-based statistics measure only the number of admissions and not the number of persons admitted. Errors in diagnosis are particularly likely to be made for rare and unusual diagnoses. This is due to lack of familiarity and information.

*Validity*: Hospital admissions and treatment demand have to be considered as limited indicators of patterns of use. Changes in these statistics can indicate an actual change in circumstances, such as changes in service provision (beds, new treatments, new treatment centres), change in the attitude of the population towards hospitalisation or treatment (refusal or acceptance of treatment in hospital, better acceptance of treatment of women and young people) and the existence of other forms of in-patient care.

*Relevance*: Hospital-based information appears to be a useful indicator of drug misuse trends, but is influenced by individual and medical attitudes towards treatment and treatment services, on admission policies and health care services and on attitudes to and awareness of drug misuse and related morbidity.

Apart from demand for treatment for addiction, reasons for hospitalisation, as indicators of excessive consumption, are specific to the type of drug. For alcohol, the reasons for general or psychiatric hospitalisation are: 'Alcoholism'/alcohol dependence syndrome, liver cirrhosis, acute alcohol intoxication and alcoholic psychosis (Chick 1982, Giesbrecht *et al.* 1983).

Reasons for hospital admissions associated with tobacco are heart disease, trachea, bronchial or lung cancer, and chronic obstructive lung diseases (Chandler 1986). Hospital admissions associated with prescribed psychoactive drugs (such as benzodiazepines) include parasuicide (suicide attempts) and accidental drug poisoning (Kreitman 1977). For illicit drugs hospital admissions may be recorded as overdose, hepatitis and AIDS (Plant 1987, Robertson 1987). Most illicit drug users who seek 'treatment' are heavy opiate users. The International Classification of Diseases takes account, not only of the types of drugs of dependence, but also of the non-dependent abuse of drugs (World Health Organization 1977).

*b. Community-based data.* Out-patient clinics provide information on addicts who request help in changing their consumption habits, either on advice or on personal initiative. Such requests are usually made by excessive or regular consumers. However, the demand for addiction treatment greatly depends on the drug used and on the extent to which the patients are aware of their addiction and of the physical or psychological risk involved. The demand for treatment also reflects the general social context. Moreover, the same patient may request help on several occasions, so this population is in no way representative of drug users.

Data provided by general practitioners relate to wider populations of drug users and may include irregular and regular consumers who have not yet had problems with psychoactive drugs. Drug abusers, incidentally, may rarely consult a doctor. Doctors are aware of practically all pharmaceutical drug users since they issue the prescriptions. General practitioners can provide useful information on users from both a clinical and social perspective. Clinicians may have very little idea of the extent of 'drug' problems amongst those for whom they prescribe (Hartnoll *et al.* 1985, Ministère de Affaires Sociales et de la Solidarité Nationale et au Secretariate d'Etat Charge' de la Santé 1985, Robertson 1987).

*Availability*: The availability of such data is limited and depends on the health care service of the country concerned. Out-patient clinic information may be available only at a local level. Availability depends on the willingness of clinics to provide it, so overall data are not easy to obtain.

*Reliability*: The data are reliable with regard to expressed demand or request for treatment.

*Validity*: The validity of these data depends on the system for recording them and also on patients' attitudes (i.e. whether they are informed about methods of treatment, whether they consult easily or not), on health care policies, and on advertising for treatment centres or for special treatment.

*Relevance*: These data provide information on drug use and also on how drug consumers make use of treatment services. The demand for treatment depends on the availability of services and upon other factors such as social status, sex and educational level of the patient.

General practitioners are the best source of information for users of prescribed psychoactive drugs. The information that they can provide with regard to users of other licit drugs depends on: (1) The extent to which consumers consult (heavy users tend to do so more than do those who use small amounts); (2) The truthfulness of patients regarding their level of consumption (particularly problematic in the case of alcohol and illicit drugs (Playoust and Zylberg 1980).

## Prescription and Retail Pharmacy Data

Prescription data indicate the amount of medicine made available to the general public (Caisse Nationale de l'Assurance Malades des Travailleurs Salariés 1985). These data can be obtained from hospitals and by direct consultation with general practitioners and specialists. Through retail pharmacists the quantity of medicine purchases, and therefore effectively available, compared to the quantity prescribed, can be established (Got 1986). Moreover, retail pharmacists supply a wide variety of psychoactive ingredients which are available without prescription. Sales records provide information on categories of medicine and brand names. These are classified according to prescription or sales and not according to individuals (Données Sociales 1984).

*Availability*: Detailed prescription data are not easily accessible at a national level. In some countries this information can be obtained only through special surveys for one or more periods. For reasons of commercial sensitivity it is usually impossible to obtain information about specific brands.

*Reliability*: Data on the availability of legal psychoactive substances are reliable, but those related to consumption are less so.

*Validity*: Prescription and retail data can be valid indicators of trends in psychoactive drug availability, but they give no information about specific forms of misuse or large prescriptions for some types of drugs. They probably overestimate current drug consumption in the community because large quantities of medicine are discarded by consumers due to the non-observance of medical advice.

*Relevance*: These data can be useful for monitoring the availability of prescribed or non-prescribed licit psychoactive drugs. However, they do not indicate the incidence or prevalence of drug taking, the medical characteristics of the drug taking population, or the medical or non-medical use of these drugs.

## Police and Court Statistics

Data provided by the police and the courts concern only recorded illegal behaviour. With respect to drug use, the following behaviour is liable to prosecution: (a) Problematic alcohol intoxication (drunken driving, public drunkenness); (b) Illicit drug-related indicators (seizures, arrests and prison sentences connected with drug use or drug traffic).

Such data depend not only on the severity of the law, which is subject to change, but also on the degree to which the laws is enforced. Crime statistics can be useful, but only if police practices and priorities are taken into account. It should be noted that this information reflects not only differential police practices, but also the differential vulnerability of substance users. Some categories of people, such as foreigners, youngsters and 'deviants', may be more likely than others to attract police attention. Other categories of people, such as women and professionals may receive less attention. This social filter varies from one country to another. In all cases, when comparing such data, great care should be taken with regard to times and localities because: (a) Changes can occur in legislation or criminal law; (b) Methods of determining problematic drug use may change (e.g. blood alcohol tests).

*Availability*: These statistics are collected on a national level but are not easily accessible.

*Reliability*: In principle the data are reliable but more information is needed on: (a) How data are collected; (b) How data are recorded and published.

*Validity*: In general, the validity of these statistics is low because they do not measure excessive drug consumption.

*Relevance*: These statistics can be considered useful for monitoring or assessing drug use only when combined with other data.

Among licit drugs, only alcohol is likely often to lead to acts constituting punishable offences. These are exemplified by drunken driving and public drunkenness. In some countries it is illegal to sell tobacco to people below a certain age. Because of the criteria, such as blood alcohol levels and social factors, which are used in different contexts to define 'alcohol misuse' these statistics are commonly not comparable from one period to another and from one country to another. Moreover, the rate of recorded offences varies greatly according to the country and the social acceptability of the substance. An increase (or decrease) in these indices may indicate a change in policy leading to greater (or lesser) availability of police officers and more (or less) rigid enforcement of the law.

Since the production, sale and possession of illicit drugs are by definition prohibited, rates for their procurement and use can only be indirectly inferred through seizures, arrests and prison sentences.

Many arrests result in convictions. Even so, arrest reflects the time at which a person is apprehended, whereas conviction relates to a court decision. Such data can provide information about the availability of illicit drugs, but, because of local involvement of police, they can only be considered as indicative of drug use.

Seizures by police and customs indicate general trends and sometimes give an indication of the size of a market or of a supply network. However, seizures are strongly influenced by opportunities and by the efficiency of the authorities concerned. The amount of drugs seized can help to assess demand. Nevertheless, caution is required in interpreting such evidence, since the eventual destination of the drugs seized and of drug distribution networks are not always known: sometimes the drug is only in transit and is not intended for the local population. The number of custodial sentences for drug offences reflects not only the offence rate but also court policies.

## Economic Statistics

Information concerning the production and sales of alcohol, tobacco and psychoactive drugs is available in most countries (Lebrun and Berlot 1983, Lamielle 1984, Chandler 1986, Got 1986). These data generally serve to assess consumption rates, which are published annually in the form of averages per inhabitant, without distinction of age or averages per inhabitant over a specific age such as 15. In fact, production and sales figures measure the availability and not the consumption of substances. Such figures can be considered as equivalent to those for alcohol and tobacco, but not to those for prescribed medicines. These statistics can be used to measure the consumption of a country, but not of a region or area, since sales do not always correspond to local consumption and vary according to regions and to season. In no circumstances do they provide information on the prevalence and incidence of consumption rates nor on consumer characteristics such as age, sex and social or psychological traits.

*Availability*: These statistics are readily available at a national and local level.

*Reliability*: They are reasonably reliable.

*Validity*: They are more valid in relation to alcohol and tobacco consumption than in relation to psychotropic medicines since many of the latter are probably discarded by consumers.

*Relevance*: These statistics are good indicators of drug use trends.

*Alcohol statistics*. They can be expressed in: (a) Litres of pure alcohol; (b) Litres of specific beverage type (beer, wines, spirits).

Beverages vary considerably in relation to their alcohol content. In France, where a profusion of alcoholic beverages is available, these statistics are not easy to interpret.

*Tobacco statistics*. These are generally expressed in the number of manufactured cigarettes, but there are differences between different types of cigarettes (e.g. filter or non-filter), and in tar and nicotine percentages. Such differences are rarely taken into account.

*Psychoactive medicine statistics*. They can be expressed in the number of pills or boxes, but it is difficult to base consumption data on these.

## DIRECT STATISTICS ON DRUG CONSUMPTION IN THE COMMUNITY

Survey data are used to determine the occurrence of drug use in the population as a whole or amongst specific subgroups. The methods used are broadly those of survey research in general. It is important to distinguish between:

1. *Household surveys concerning expenditure*. In many countries such surveys are carried out at regular intervals every year. Tobacco and alcohol are generally considered as common consumer products. Data may be elicited from the head of the family, the housewife or any adult member of the household. These surveys provide information on family rather than individual consumption rates (Robins 1977, Données Sociales 1984, Hartnoll *et al.* 1985).

2. *Population surveys of personal consumption rates*. 'Consumption' can involve the prevalence of consumption rates, previous year's consumption rates, or current consumption rates. They can measure low consumption (occasion, experimental and non-dependent use) or heavy consumption (regular consumption or abuse)(Robins 1977).

The number of cigarettes smoked daily is a fairly good indicator of consumption. Rates vary little for heavy smokers but can be significant for irregular users. Exact alcohol consumption, as already noted by Jasinski, is more difficult to assess. Apart from the variety of available beverages which is often very great in alcohol producing countries, it is difficult to cover all occasions for consumption (during or outside mealtimes, on workdays or rest days, on special occasions, etc.) and to measure the quantities consumed. In addition, consumption may be regular and controlled, or heavy and dependent, which increases the risk of accidents. Because of the different patterns of alcohol use, alcohol consumption is very difficult to determine (Chick 1982). It is difficult, particularly in the case of youngsters, to obtain the names of drugs and the exact amounts taken. In addition, therapeutic advice is not always followed. Surveys on illicit drugs are best able to measure occasional or experimental use. This is because heavy users of illicit drugs are often geographically mobile and live on the fringe of society. This makes them difficult to contact, and such people may also be suspicious of surveys since their behaviour is illegal.

*Availability*: Most countries publish official data about alcohol and tobacco consumption but the criteria used to determine consumption rates are not always the same, even within a single country, so it is difficult to compare available data.

*Reliability*: The reliability of data is greater for socially acceptable drugs than for illicit or unacceptable drugs. Reliability also depends on the respondent (self-reported consumption or consumption of a member of the family), and on his or her age and comprehension of the question.

*Validity*: The validity of the conclusions depends on:
• sample size: some drug use is very rare. The lower the frequency, the more difficult it is to measure, so the study of illicit drug use or the heavy use of legal drugs requires a very large selection of people in order to result in acceptable sample sizes.
• sampling frame: 'random' samples may be based on biased registers. The key group is often missing from such lists. For example, sampling based on election registers results in under-representation of heavy drinkers or drug users. Being on an electoral register implies a conformist lifestyle.
• methods of data collection: the questionnaire is sometimes a better method than the personal interview.

•it can be difficult to talk about consumption and easier to complete an anonymous questionnaire. Some questions can also be difficult to understand or to answer.

•non-response rate: the non-response rate depends on:

•the data collection method chosen

•the social acceptability of the drug studied (higher for tobacco and psychoactive medicines than for alcohol or illicit drugs)

•the consumption rate of the respondent (heavy users or abusers are more often in hospital, in prison or in the street looking for drugs).

*Relevance*: It appears that the relevance of these data is higher for: (a) low consumers than for heavy consumers; (b) licit than for illicit drugs; (c) younger than for older people.

*Alcohol consumption.* Consumption rates are expressed in 'glasses' (or 'units') of the beverage considered (beer, wine, spirits – in France 'aperitifs' or 'digestifs' – and other local alcoholic beverages). Because of different alcohol contents it is difficult to determine the accurate alcohol consumption of the target population. Patterns of alcohol consumption are also different (regular, irregular but heavy use, intoxication) which further complicates determining alcohol consumption.

*Tobacco consumption.* Consumption rates are expressed in the number of cigarettes smoked per day. Since irregular smoking is less frequent, statistics on consumption are relatively accurate.

*Psychoactive medicines.* These data are difficult to obtain. Young people often do not remember the name of the pharmaceutical substance or the purpose of its use. In addition, treatment directions are not always followed.

*Illicit drug consumption.* Survey research probably gives an accurate measure of low consumption ('occasional' or 'experimental' use). Non-random studies are probably better at examining heavy drug consumption. The range of 'official data' available as indicators of psychoactive drug use in the community is indicated by Table 10:1.

## Discussion

It seems that each indicator relates to only one aspect of drug use or misuse. Production and sales data and retail pharmacist and prescription data are indicators of the *availability* of licit drugs; mortality data, hospital statistics and out-patient clinic statistics are the *medical indicators of problematic drug use*. Several indicators, therefore, need to be considered in conjunction in order to

Table 10.1. Official data available to indicate patterns of psychoactive drug use in the community

| | Mortality data | Indirect indicator | | | | | Direct indicator |
|---|---|---|---|---|---|---|---|
| | | Morbidity data | | Prescription and retail pharmacy data | Police and court statistics | Economic statistics | |
| | | Hospital based | Community based | | | | |
| Alcohol consumption | 'Alcoholism'/alcohol dependence Cirrhosis Acute alcohol intoxication Alcoholic psychosis | General hospital – diagnosis – treatment demand Pyschiatric hospital diagnosis | GP* Out-patient treatment centres | | Drunken driving records Public drunkenness | Production and sales data | Population surveys Medical care centres |
| Tobacco consumption | Lung trachea bronchial cancer Ischaemic heart disease | General hospital – diagnosis – treatment demand | GP Out-patient treatment centres | | | Production and sales data | Population surveys Medical care centres |
| Licit psychoactive substances | Suicide Accidental poisoning by drug | General hospital (emergency, suicide attempts) Psychiatric hospital (depression, mental illness) | GP | GPs and psychiatrists' prescriptions Retail pharmacists | | Product data | Population surveys Medical care centres |
| Illicit psychoactive substances | Overdose AIDS | General hospital – diagnosis – treatment demand | GP Out-patient treatment centres | | Arrests Seizure Customs Imprisonment | | Population surveys Multisource enumeration case finding |

* General practitioner.

107

assess drug use and misuse rates with any degree of rigor. Official records rarely produce a sample of people representative of all users. Different data become valuable when they are collected over a number of years, and may indicate and reflect trends over a long period.

Indirect indicators have the enormous *advantage* of being available at minimal cost, of having been systematically collected for some time, of being easily accessible and of being usable on a national or local scale. Nevertheless, the *disadvantage* of these indicators must not be overlooked: they only relate to some of the harmful consequences of drug use or of the availability of drugs to the general public. They give only very simple and minimal information (i.e. sex, age, diagnosis). They reflect the priorities and policies of the bodies that provide information. They are invariably purely quantitative. In addition, they measure events (except for mortality!) rather than individual behaviour, and so do not necessarily indicate the number of people concerned.

However, these indicators are often overlooked in preference to studies that are more costly, complicated and difficult to implement. Although surveys make it possible to measure consumption more accurately among the general population and to examine individual patterns of drug use, they are not without their disadvantages. For example, as elaborated elsewhere in this book (Chapters 1 and 2) drug use can be over- or under-reported according to the age of the respondent, to his or her attitude to different drugs and to the method used for data collection. Moreover, the non-response rate is sometimes high and is related to data collection methods (such as face to face or telephone interviews, mail questionnaires), to the drug studied (social acceptability differs for licit and illicit drugs) and to the population sampled (deviants are less likely to respond). In addition, representative random samples are difficult to obtain and are often based on electoral registers or other biased frames.

This review indicates that the validity of data largely depends on the stability of the monitoring system, on the attitudes of experts and drug users in terms of social and medical care provided, and on the social, legal and medical policies for tackling drug problems. Discrepancies obviously exist between different periods and areas, and particularly between different countries. A comparison of international data is not always possible, and attempts to determine comparative rates of consumption should proceed with extreme caution.

As a first step, a useful contribution would be for *each country* to compile: (1) A list of the sources of available data; (2) A definition of their content, their method of collection and their origin; (3) An estimate of their reliability and their validity.

These steps could be the *preparation* for an international comparison. In any case, it is a *necessary* step towards standardizing the nature and sources of data on an international scale.

REFERENCES

Caisse Nationale de l'Assurance Malades des Travailleurs Salariés (1985) *Qnquête Morbidité Prescriptions Pharmaceutiques Novembre 1982–November 1983*, Paris, Caisse National de l'Assurance Malades des Travailleurs.

Chandler, W.U. (1986) *Banishing Tobacco*, Worldwatch Institute Paper 68.

Chick, J. (1982) Epidemiology of alcohol use and its hazards, *British Medical Bulletin* 38, 3–8.

Données Sociales (1984) National Institute of Statistics and Economic Studies.

Giesbrecht, N., Cahannes, M., Moskalewicz, J., Österberg, E. and Room, R. (1983) *Consequences of Drinking. Trends in Alcohol Problem Statistics in Seven Countries*, Toronto: Addiction Research Foundation.

Got, I. (1986) *Les Indicateurs Nationaux et Régionaux de L'Alcoolisation en France*, Thèse de Médicine, Université Paris V.

Hartnoll, R., Daviaud, E., Lewis, R. and Mitcheson, M. (1985) *Drug Problems: Assessing Local Needs*, London: Drug Indicators Project, Department of Politics and Sociology, University of London.

Kreitman, N. (1977) *Parasuicide*, Wiley: Chichester.

Lamielle, D. (1984) *Evolution de la Consommation de Cigarettes en France et dans le Monde*, SEITA.

Lebrun, G. and Berlot, J.M. (1983) *Analyse Critique des Bases de Données sur la Consommation de Boissons Alcoolisées*. Rapport de stage DESS: Gestion des Services de Santé, Université Paris-Dauphine.

Ministère des Affaires Sociales et de la Solidarité (1984) *Solidarité–Santé. Etudes statistiques*. Ministère des Affaires Sociales et de la Solidarité, Documentation Française, Paris, 1,2.

Ministère des Affaires Sociales et de la Solidarité Nationale et au Secretariat d'Etat chargéde La Santé (1985) *La Santé en France*, Rapport au Ministre des Affaires Sociales et de la Solidarité Nationale et au Secretariat d'Etat chargé de La Santé. Documentation Française, Paris, Coll. des rapports officiels.

Plant, M.A. (1987) *Drugs in Perspective*, London: Hodder and Stoughton.

Playoust, D. and Zylberg, G. (1980) Tentative de définition de l'alcoolisation d'une population. *Bulletin de la SFA*, No. 2.

Robertson, J.R. (1987) *Heroin, AIDS and Society*, London: Hodder and Stoughton.

Robins, L.N., (1977) Surveys of target populations. In Richards, I., Louise, G. and Blevens, L.B. *The Epidemiology of Drug Abuse: Current Issues*. Rockville, Maryland: National Institute on Drug Abuse.

Royal College of Physicians (1983) *Health or Smoking?* London: Pitman.

# 11. The Relationship Between Consumption Patterns of Alcohol, Tobacco, Prescribed and Illegal Drugs and Harmful Consequences

ANNA KOKKEVI and COSTAS STEFANIS

*Abstract.* An overview of current research methods in the drug use field is briefly presented. This is followed by a description of two Greek studies aiming to examine epidemiological aspects of substance use. The two populations, one in an early and another in an advanced stage of drug use career, were investigated by different methods. These respondents (students and imprisoned drug dependents) showed a pattern of increased substance dependency with a wider range of substances used. Problems which affected the physical and mental health as well as social functioning of imprisoned drug dependents were also evident amongst student drug takers, especially those who had used heroin. Several methodological issues related to the assessment of drug use and misuse are discussed.

## Introduction

Research on licit and illicit substance use and abuse has flourished in the past two decades due to increased public and governmental concern about their harmful effects on the individual and society. A wide spectrum of research issues has been examined, ranging from the prevalence and patterns of licit and illicit substance use, to aetiology and consequences of drug use. It is generally acknowledged that the information derived from such studies is a necessary, but not a sufficient, condition for formulating and implementing legal and social policies to prevent the spreading epidemic of substance dependence. The methods employed in obtaining reliable and valid information on the various aspects of substance use are thus important. This chapter addresses this issue by a critical review of the methods currently employed in substance use research, and by presenting data on patterns and consequences of drug use obtained in two Greek studies. These adopted different methods and related to two study groups, one in an early and the other in an advanced phase, of drug-use career.

## CURRENT METHODS

Many cross-sectional surveys of general populations or subgroups, such as students and military conscripts, have been conducted (Johnston 1980, Smart, Hughes, Johnston, Anumonye, Khant, Medina-Mora, Navaratnam, Poshyachinda, Varma and Wadud 1980). Such exercises have been carried out either by home visits and personal or telephone interviews or by mailed self-administered questionnaires. In this type of study large samples are needed, particularly if substance use is not widespread, or if relevant information stems from representative sub-populations, such as those from specific geographical regions or from certain age groups. Household surveys may not locate people without a permanent residence. Drug users, especially heroin dependents, are likely to be in this category. Moreover, surveys by personal interview are, compared to mailed questionnaires, quite costly, and potential respondents may be concerned about preserving their anonymity. Conversely, the likelihood of respondents failing to comprehend questions and to provide inaccurate answers is considerably reduced with the direct person-to-person interview. Direct interviewing achieves higher response rates than do most mailed questionnaire approaches (Hughes, Jarvis, Khant, Medina-Mora, Navaratnam, Poshyachinda and Wadud 1982, Johnston 1982).

School surveys have several advantages. Data may be obtained from respondents in groups (classrooms) by anonymous self-administered questionnaires. By this approach large samples may be studied and a higher level of truthful answering might be attained. Since illicit drug use is especially commonplace among adolescents and young adults, the number of users within such samples can be large enough to study the correlates of use, even of the less common substances. Moreover, the cost of such surveys is comparatively low. However, school surveys do not reach those who have left school or have dropped out of the educational system. Such people may be especially likely to use drugs, particularly illegal drugs (Johnston and O'Malley 1984).

General population and school surveys provide useful information for the direction of policy on prevention and treatment, by assessing overall levels of substance use and by identifying high-risk groups. Repetition of cross-sectional surveys is required to provide information on trends in the use of known substances and on the possible emergence of new substances. Follow-up studies are also necessary to monitor the effectiveness of policies in the field of prevention.

Case studies (ethnographic surveys of known cases) of samples of drug abusers, based on retrospective methods, can yield information on causal factors as well as on user careers and on the sequential order and consequences of drug use (Hughes, Venulet, Khant, Medina-Mora, Navaratnam, Poshyachinda, Rootman, Salan and Wadud 1980). More reliable and valid answers to all these questions can be obtained by longitudinal and cohort studies which are of long duration and are expensive (Kandel 1978).

Another method, largely employed to study the consequences of drug use, is the processing of information obtained from records of treatment services and law enforcement agencies (Rootman and Hughes, 1980). As noted in the previous chapter, the validity (accuracy) of information from these sources is often dubious.

A number of factors affecting the validity of information obtained by each of the above methods have been identified and will briefly be discussed.

a. *The type of substance used.* Its legal status in the given country and/or the social reaction to its use: The more rigidly controlled the substance is, the more reluctant the respondent will be to admitting its use.

b. *The age of the population surveyed and the stage of involvement with drugs.* Young people at an early stage of involvement with drugs that are illicit or which are not viewed as suitable for those of their age may be wary of admitting to the use of such substances. The opposite is true for older users and particularly for those already identified as 'cases' of drug abuse.

c. *The type of the organisation conducting the survey* (e.g. university, health agency, police) as well as the setting or locality in which the survey takes place (respondent's residence, school, military setting): This undoubtedly influences the degree of respondents' trust in the interviewers, and consequently the validity of self-reporting. Conscripts surveyed in a military setting or adolescents in their parental homes may feel insecure about admitting the use of substances or any behaviours not acceptable in their social context.

d. *The survey technique used.* Personal face-to-face interview versus telephone interview or anonymous self-administered questionnaire. Methods have been developed to guarantee anonymity of answers related to drug use in a person-to-person interview, for example, using written answer sheets which the respondent either seals in an envelope and hands to the interviewer or mails to the research agency. Even so, the interview situation may affect truthful reporting, especially in certain age groups, mainly the young. Several studies comparing the validity of results obtained from named and anonymous respondents about self-reported drug use have indicated that little or no difference exists between the two approaches (King 1970, Luetgert and Haberman 1973, Hochhauser 1979, Needle, McCubbin, Lorence and Hochhauser 1983). Validity of reporting may, however, vary according to the legal status of the substance used, the socio-cultural context of its use and the age of respondents (Dube, Kumar, Gupta and Kumar 1981, Benson and Holberg 1985, Johnston and O'Malley 1984).

e. *The design of instruments employed for data collection.* Two major aspects of the instrument structure may influence reliability and validity of answers. Firstly, the clarity of drug-related questions (for example, definitions of drug classes: giving examples of 'street names'; clear differentiation between medically and non-medically used substances, self medication versus recreational use; well-defined categories of frequency of use; age of first use etc.). Secondly, the general presentation of the instrument and its purpose. If, for example, the instrument includes questions on health-related matters or lifestyles, and is not focused exclusively on drug use, it is possible that it will reduce under-reporting or over-reporting. Some evidence suggests that disguising interview schedules has little effect on self-reports (Plant and Miller 1977).

f. *The national and/or local general conditions not directly related to the substance use.* This is a factor that has to be taken into account in all methods. Its influence upon the validity of the results may be illustrated with reference to its effect on sample representativeness. The response rate in a survey may vary from one country to another for the same method, according to local factors. Mailed self-administered questionnaires, for example, used to survey the general population, may have very low response rates in countries in which the average educational level of the population is low. On the contrary, the response rate of schools may be high in countries in which participation is decided upon by the Ministry of Education, and not at the level of each school's administration.

THE GREEK EXPERIENCE

## The Local Scene

Increasing consumption of licit and illicit substance use was noted towards the end of the 1970s in Greece among the young people. Moreover, patterns of use amongst young people seemed also to have changed. The young steadily moved away from traditional drug use confined to alcohol and tobacco (Stefanis, Ballas and Madianou 1977).

The spread of substance use, and in particular that of illicit drugs among young people, generated public and political concern. Collection of scientific data on the extent and nature of this phenomenon was felt to be necessary in order to guide social policy and the planning of preventive programmes.

Two studies were undertaken by Athens University Medical School within the frame of a larger epidemiological investigation on the prevalence and patterns of substance use and psychosocial factors contributing to drug initiation and drug seeking behaviour.

## Study Groups and Methods

Data were collected within the same year from a representative school population sample (in Spring 1984) and imprisoned drug dependents (April–July 1984).

The school study was a cross-sectional survey conducted on a nationwide stratified sample. Students (N = 11, 058) completed an anonymous self-administered questionnaire in their classrooms. Trained field workers conducted the survey, and no teacher was present in the classroom during data collection.

The survey instrument included a wide range of questions related to life style, personality, behaviour, attitudes, school and family background. The main part of the questionnaire included items related to tobacco, alcohol, prescribed drugs taken with and without prescription and illicit drugs. Lifetime, 12-months and 30-day prevalence of use were examined. Availability of substances, drug use by friends, circumstances of first use, problems resulting from the use and attitudes towards licit and illicit drugs were also investigated. The questionnaire was presented to the students as an examination of their psychosocial needs.

Reliability, internal consistency and validity of the drug use related answers were checked through a pilot study conducted four months before the main study within the same school year. Validity was checked by internal and external criteria, including urine tests to detect drug use. Both reliability and validity of self-reported drug use proved to be very high.

The study of imprisoned drug addicts was carried out with a sample of 79 males in the psychiatric section of the Athens prison; these individuals had been imprisoned for drug offences. Substance abuse diagnosis was cross-checked by criteria based on the *American Psychiatric Association's Diagnostic and Statistical Manual of Mental Disorders* (DSM-III). The sample was representative of the imprisoned drug addicts in Greece. Out of the total target sample only one subject refused the interview, while another was unable to co-operate. A group of 57 imprisoned non-drug-dependents matched for sex, age and duration of present imprisonment was used as a control group.

Subjects were interviewed by clinical psychologists and psychiatrists, using a series of psychological and psychiatric instruments. An extensive structured interview included, among others, questions on the life history, 12 months and 30 days prior to imprisonment, use of tobacco, alcohol, prescribed drugs used with and without a doctor's prescription and illicit drugs. A large number of additional items on psychological and social variables related to drug use and attitudes were also part of the interview.

Subjects had a mean age of 30 years. They had received an average of 8.5 mean years of school education. In both groups subjects mainly belonged to lower socio-economic groups and had been born and were resident in the greater Athens area.

## Patterns of Substance Use

In order to acquire a better understanding of possible relationships between the use of different substances as well as between drug use and its adverse psychosocial consequences, students were grouped according to their reported use of licit and illicit substances. Eight categories of respondent were distinguished: (1) No regular use of any licit and not at all of any illicit substance (44.7 per cent); (2) Smoking regularly (8.4 per cent); (3) Drinking alcohol regularly but not smoking (8.6 per cent); (4) Smoking and drinking alcohol regularly (6.8 per cent); (5) Have used one or two types of licit psychotropic drugs without prescription (2.8 per cent); (6) Have used three or more types of licit psychotropic drugs without prescription (2.8%); (7) Have used illicit drugs, except heroin (5.5 per cent); (8) Have used heroin (0.5 per cent). Each subject was placed in one of the above categories according to the highest ranking substance that he or she had used.

The imprisoned drug dependents were polydrug users, with

heroin being the main substance of abuse. They had used a mean of 4.1 types of illicit drugs (these included glues and solvents). They had also used on average 6.2 out of the eight categories of drugs for which a prescription is required. The mean duration of illicit drug use was 13.6 years. Almost half of the study group (48.9 per cent), had a lifetime diagnosis of alcoholism according to DSM-III criteria. Regular tobacco use was reported by all subjects. Only two individuals reported having stopped smoking.

The findings from both population groups provided evidence of a progressively heavier consumption of lower ranking licit or illicit drugs (such as cannabis and alcohol) as subjects were getting more and more involved in the use of higher ranking drugs (such as cocaine and opiates).

More specifically, amongst the students it was found that the use of tobacco and alcohol as well as of psychotropic drugs obtained without prescription was significantly heavier amongst those who had used the widest range of illicit drugs. Students who had used heroin had all used cannabis (marihuana) or some other illicit drug, while 82.5 per cent had used licit psychotropic drugs without prescription. Almost all (96.5 per cent) were tobacco smokers and alcohol users (94.7 per cent). Most were regular smokers (64.9 per cent) and heavy drinkers (68.4 per cent).

Imprisoned addicts who could be considered as having entered the final stage of a drug career had used almost all types of licit drugs and most continued to be polydrug users prior to imprisonment. Heavy tobacco smoking was an obvious feature of the entire group. Alcohol consumption appeared to be 'heavy' amongst approximately a quarter of the study group, who reported daily consumption exceeding five glasses of alcohol.

## Problems Related to Patterns of Substance Use

Multiple drug use and drug dependence was found to have consequences not only on physical health but also on the psychological and social functioning of the individual.

As shown in the student study, the rates of reported health problems, parasuicides (suicide attempts) and law violations significantly increased with progressive involvement with licit and more especially illicit drug use, peaking in the heroin use category. This is shown by Figures 11.1, 11.2 and 11.3.

The problems depicted by these figures are only some of a much wider range of psychological and social problems which were examined in this study. They are consistent with the conclusion

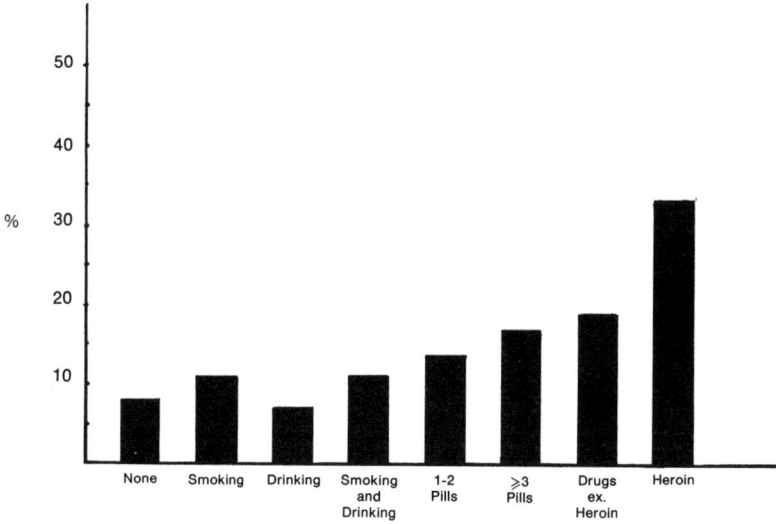

Figure 11.1. Rates of students reporting health problems in the usage variable groups

that 'problems' are associated with heavier levels of psychoactive drug use.

The increasing level of adverse consequences on physical and

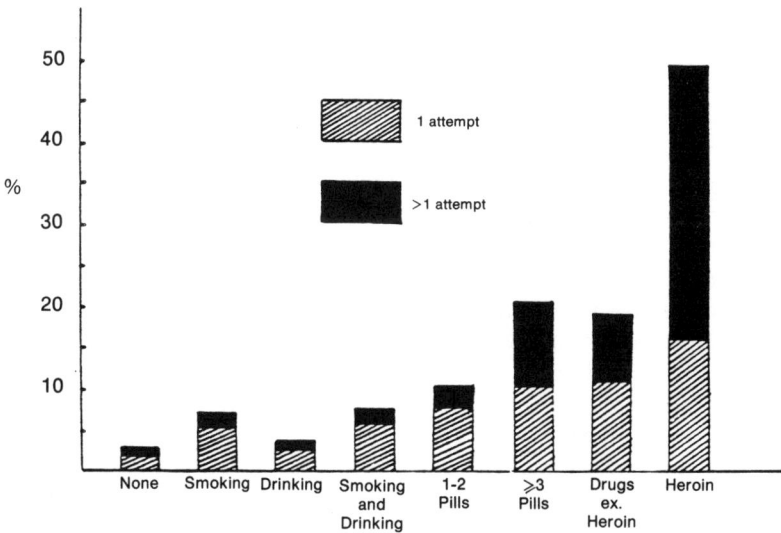

Figure 11.2. Rates of students reporting suicide attempts in the usage variable groups

117

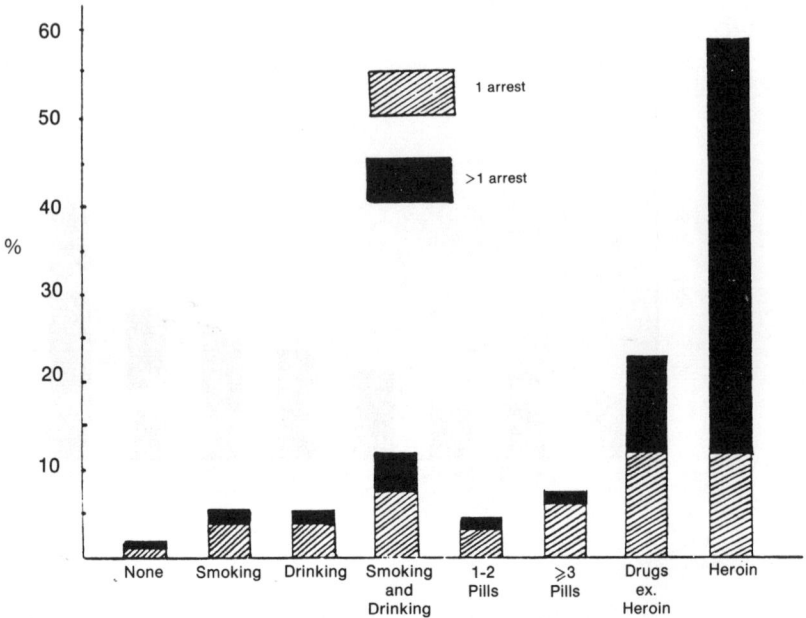

Figure 11.3. Rates of students reporting police arrests in the usage variable groups

psychosocial health as a function of degree of involvement with licit or illicit substances is further illustrated in Table 11.1. This presents data on self-reported problems related to alcohol use. Alcohol-related problems increase as one progresses from regular alcohol use to the additional use of other licit and illicit substances, with the exception of the 1–2 pills category. It is further shown that cumulative substance use was associated with higher rate of alcohol-related problems among the illicit drug users than was evident among those who were moderate and heavy drinkers. By classifying the students according to their alcohol consumption levels (1 = non or very light, 2 = light, 3 = moderate and 4 = heavy) it was found that absence of any alcohol-related problems was reported by 73.4 per cent of students in the 1st, 57.9 per cent in the 2nd, 42.2 per cent in the 3rd and 28.5 per cent in the 4th alcohol consumption groups. As shown in Table 11.1 the respective means in the substance usage variable categories dropped from 50.5 per cent in the 'drinking only' (moderate and heavy drinkers) group to 17.6 per cent in the last category of heroin users.

As shown in Table 11.2, 74.7 per cent of the imprisoned drug

Table 11.1. Rates of self-reported alcohol related problems amongst students

| Alcohol-Related Problems | Usage Variable Categories | | | | | |
|---|---|---|---|---|---|---|
| | Drinking | Smoking and Drinking | Pills 1-2 | Pills ≥3 | Drugs Except Heroin | Heroin |
| | % | % | % | % | % | % |
| Caused you to behave in ways that you later regretted | 17.4 | 25.4 | 18.5 | 28.7 | 34.2 | 23.5 |
| Hurt your relationship with your parents | 7.2 | 11.7 | 7.4 | 16.7 | 16.8 | 33.3 |
| Hurt your relationships with your friends | 4.1 | 8.2 | 5.9 | 8.9 | 14.8 | 13.7 |
| Hurt your relationships with teachers or supervisors | 1.1 | 2.8 | 0.9 | 3.2 | 3.6 | 9.8 |
| Involved you with people you think are a bad influence on you | 5.2 | 10.6 | 5.3 | 9.6 | 9.2 | 17.6 |
| Hurt your performance in school and/or on the job | 5.3 | 7.0 | 5.7 | 18.5 | 11.4 | 17.6 |
| Caused you to be less interested in other activities than you were before | 3.0 | 4.6 | 3.9 | 7.1 | 8.3 | 11.8 |
| Caused you to be less stable emotionally | 20.7 | 21.8 | 22.9 | 35.1 | 33.3 | 35.3 |
| Caused you to have less energy | 10.1 | 9.6 | 9.7 | 11.3 | 13.0 | 7.8 |
| Interfered with your ability to think clearly | 18.8 | 21.6 | 19.7 | 24.8 | 27.2 | 25.5 |
| Caused you problems of attention and memory | 9.2 | 8.7 | 8.8 | 13.1 | 11.2 | 15.7 |
| Had other bad psychological effects | 3.3 | 4.5 | 4.4 | 11.0 | 11.2 | 11.8 |
| Caused your physical health to be bad | 6.3 | 10.9 | 8.7 | 16.7 | 13.2 | 19.6 |
| Lead you into trouble with the police | 1.0 | 2.8 | 0.6 | 3.2 | 7.4 | 29.4 |
| Caused you to drive unsafely | 4.7 | 18.0 | 4.6 | 8.5 | 21.3 | 43.1 |
| Caused you none of the above problems | 50.5 | 38.6 | 47.7 | 25.9 | 24.1 | 17.6 |

119

Table 11.2. Rates of imprisoned drug dependents reporting illicit drug-related problems

| *Drug-Related problems* | *Imprisoned drug dependents (N = 79)* |
|---|---|
| | % |
| Caused you to behave in ways that you later regretted | 48.1 |
| Hurt your relationship with your parents | 53.2 |
| Hurt your relationships with your friends | 45.6 |
| Hurt your relationships with teachers or supervisors | 30.4 |
| Involved you with people you think have a bad influence on you | 46.8 |
| Hurt your performance in school and/or on the job | 43.0 |
| Lost your job | 26.6 |
| Caused you to be less interested in other activities than you were before | 44.3 |
| Caused you to be less stable emotionally | 51.9 |
| Caused you to have less energy | 39.2 |
| Interfered with your ability to think clearly | 39.2 |
| Had other bad psychological effects | 38.0 |
| Caused your physical health to be bad | 45.6 |
| Caused you problems of attention and memory | 35.4 |
| Caused you overdose episodes | 24.1 |
| Caused you to drive unsafely | 25.3 |
| Hurt your relationships with your spouse, fiancee, or girlfriend/boyfriend | 40.5 |
| Led you into trouble with the police | 62.0 |
| Other problems | 17.7 |

dependents reported having experienced severe consequences during their long drug user careers. Most of these individuals reported adverse legal consequences (62.0 per cent), and poor family relationships (53.2 per cent).

Moreover, more than a quarter of the subjects (27.8 per cent) reported having attempted suicide. In addition 68.3 per cent of them had been arrested more than three times in their lives and 50.7 per cent had been convicted more than once (62.5 per cent were sentenced for drug related offences, 30.4 per cent for acquisition crimes, 24 per cent for violent crimes and 15.8 per cent for other reasons). Comparison with the control group of imprisoned non-addicts has shown that half of the drug dependents compared with only a quarter of the controls had been convicted two or more times.

The majority of students who reported having used heroin could not be considered as dependent or heavy polydrug users.

Even so, they did share some of the characteristics of the imprisoned drug users. Students who had used illicit drugs, mainly heroin, had higher rates of health problems, suicide attempts and police arrests, compared to other students. This is shown in Figures 11.1–11.3.

The question that may be raised at this point is whether the described pattern indicates a causal relationship between progressive drug involvement and psychosocial problems (Stefanis and Kokkevi 1987) or whether it merely describes a 'syndrome of problem behaviour' associated with drug use. In the latter case drug use could be either an integral part of this global problem behaviour syndrome (Jessor and Jessor, 1980) or a manifestation of social deviance (Gordon 1983).

The two Greek studies reported above, due to their design, cannot answer this question. A prospective longitudinal study of adolescents would be necessary to identify antecedent factors to drug use and distinguish them from secondary phenomena. The results described in this chapter can nevertheless suggest a number of assumptions about this issue.

## SOME CONCLUSIONS ABOUT THE METHODOLOGICAL IMPLICATIONS OF THE GREEK EXPERIENCE

This brief description of two Greek surveys suggests that data obtained through different approaches are equally reliable and valid, provided that each method is properly designed to meet research aims and to suit the characteristics of the study group and local and/or national conditions.

In the school survey reluctance to admit 'deviant' behaviour may have been minimized, by preserving anonymity, by including in the questionnaire items not related to drug use and by carefully controlling the testing conditions. Also the fact that the involvement of schools in the research was agreed by the Ministry of Education facilitated an unbiased sampling procedure. The questionnaire design provided the opportunity to determine not only patterns of substance use, but also to obtain valuable information on correlates and consequences of such use. Counterbalancing these advantages, the school surveys undoubtedly missed some young heavy drug users who had dropped out of education.

On the other hand, the results derived from the imprisoned drug dependents showed that the personal interviews employed did not reduce either response rate or apparent willingness to report. This was due to the fact that the survey was conducted by an institution (a university) which guaranteed confidentiality of information and the subjects were all 'cases' of drug abuse, identified as such in prison records. This study provided detailed information on the correlates of drug abuse. This has limited relevance due to the atypical group studied. The scheduled extension of the study to other groups of drug dependents in treatment services or identified through the 'snowball' technique (Polsky 1969, Plant 1975) will undoubtedly increase the range of the study group. The use of a comparison group of imprisoned non-addicts made it possible at least to control for variables related to imprisonment.

Although the data presented in this chapter were obtained by two different studies, in which different population samples and methods were used, in many respects they were comparable with and complementary to each other. Both yielded a wealth of information that may serve to guide national policy on drug abuse prevention. Moreover, the experience acquired by the methods employed in these two studies in Greece may be applicable in other settings and other countries.

It is noted that some surveys limit their investigations to only one category of substances. Separate surveys are conducted for tobacco, alcohol, licit and illicit drugs. The Greek experience noted above has shown that the combined investigation of all or of many substances together during the same survey has several methodological as well as economic advantages. It allows for determining the sequence and possible inter-relationships among substances in their use and in their adverse consequences. Also, more information is provided at lower cost.

The choice of the method to be used in drug dependence research does primarily depend on the nature and priorities of the chosen objectives. However, factors such as local situation and the availability of resources often prevail over scientific considerations. Longitudinal studies are more appropriate than cross-sectional studies to investigate causal relationships and temporal issues. Nevertheless, single phase cross-cultural surveys can provide a wealth of information that can effectively be utilised for guiding social policy and preventive initiatives.

A better understanding of the multifaceted phenomenon of substance use would be achieved by utilising multiple and diverse sources of information (Hartnoll, Daviaud, Lewis and Mitcheson 1985). Deficiencies inherent in each particular method may lead to faulty interpretation of data. To illustrate, a cross validation of self-reported drug problems may be achieved by using data provided by two different populations (e.g. students, identified cases of drug abusers) and/or data obtained through services or different agencies on specific areas of interest such as accidents, morbidity, suicide or crimes.

An important issue related to data gathering procedure at local or national level is comparability of information with results obtained by similar studies within or outside the country concerned. This has been elaborated by Anokhina and Ivanets. The use of clear definitions as well as the use of a set of core questions identified as such in well-documented studies or proposed by international organisations is therefore highly recommended. Comparison of data from different studies and countries provides not only important information on the extent of substance use and related sociocultural factors at a local or national level, but also has major implications for improving research designs and for the effective planning of preventive policies.

REFERENCES

Benson, G. and Holberg, M.B. (1985) Validity of the questionnaires in population studies on drug use, *Acta Psychiatrica Scandinavica* 71, 9–18.

Dube, K.C., Kumar, A.T., Gupta, S.P. and Kumar, N. (1981) The question of onymity and anonymity of questionnaire in a drug use survey, *Bulletin of Narcotics* 36, 2, 45–8.

Gordon, A.M. (1983) Drugs and delinquency. A ten year follow-up of drug clinic patients, *British Journal of Psychiatry* 142, 169–73.

Hartnoll, R., Daviaud, E., Lewis, R. and Mitcheson, M. (1985) *Drug Problems: Assessing Local Needs*, London: Drug Indicators Project, Department of Politics and Sociology, University of London.

Hochhauser, M. (1979) Bias in drug abuse survey research, *The International Journal of the Addictions* 14, 675–87.

Hughes, P.H., Jarvis, G.K., Khant, U., Medina-Mora, M.E., Navaratnam, V., Poshyachinda, V. and Wadud, K.A. (1982) A rationale for identification of cases of drug abuse, *Bulletin of Narcotics* 34, 2, 1–14.

Hughes, P.H., Venulet, J., Khant, U., Medina-Mora, M.E., Navaratnam, V., Poshyachinda, V., Rootman, I., Salan, R. and Wadud, A. (1980) *Core Data for Epidemiological Studies of Nonmedical Drug Use*. WHO Offset Publication No. 56, Geneva: WHO.

Jessor, R. and Jessor, S. (1980) *A Social-Psychological Framework for Studying Drug Use*, Rockville, Maryland: National Institute on Drug Use Research Monograph Series, 30, 102–9.

Johnston, L.D. (1980) *Review of General Population Surveys of Drug Use*, WHO Offset Publication No. 52, Geneva: WHO.

Johnston, L.D. (1982) *The Epidemiology of Drug Use and Abuse: An Overview of the Research Policy Questions and the Methods appropriate to answering them*, Pompidou Group Document P-PG (82) 38.

Johnston, L.D. and O'Malley, P.M. (1984) *Issues on Validity and Population Coverage in Student Surveys of Drug Use*. Paper presented at a

National Institute on Drug Abuse technical review on Current Challenges to Methods of Drug Abuse Estimations and held in Bethesda, Md., 8–9 May.

Kandel, D.B. (1978) *Longitudinal Research on Drug Use*, New York: Wiley.

King, G.M. (1970) Anonymous vs. identifiable questionnaires in drug usage surveys, *American Psychologist* 25, 982–5.

Luetgert, M.J. and Haberman, A.A. (1973) Methodological issues in drug usage surveys: Anonymity, recency and frequency, *The International Journal of the Addictions* 8, 683–9.

Needle, R., McCubbin, H., Lorence, J. and Hochhauser, M. (1983) Reliability and validity of adolescent self-reported drug use in a family-based study: A methodological report, *The International Journal of the Addictions* 18, 7, 901–12.

Plant, M.A. (1975) *Drugtakers in an English Town*, London: Tavistock.

Plant, M.A. and Miller, T.I. (1977) Disguised and undisguised questionnaires compared: Two alternative approaches to drinking behaviour surveys, *Social Psychiatry* 12, 21–4.

Polsky, N. (1969) *Hustlers, Beats and Others*, Harmondsworth, Middx.: Pelican.

Rootman, I. and Hughes, P.H. (1980) *Drug-Abuse Reporting Systems*, WHO Offset Publication No. 55, Geneva: WHO.

Smart, R.G., Hughes, P.H., Johnston, L.D., Anumonye, A., Khant, U., Medina-Mora, M.E., Navaratnam, V., Poshyachinda, V., Varma, V.K. and Wadud, K.A. (1980) *A Methodology for Student Drug-Use Surveys*, WHO Offset Publication No. 50, Geneva: WHO

Stefanis, C.N., Ballas, C. and Madianou, D. (1977) Sociocultural aspects of hashish use in Greece. In Stefanis, C., Dornbush, R. and Fink, M. (eds) *Hashish Studies of Long-term Use*, pp. 1–9, New York, Raven Press.

Stefanis, C.N. and Kokkevi, A. (1986) Depression and drug use, *Psychopathology* 19, 124–31.

# 12. Polydrug Abuse: Standards For Comparative Measures

WOLFRAM KEUP

*Abstract.* This chapter describes three methods of recording information on patterns of multiple drug abuse in three studies. Each of them is based upon large unselected patient populations drawn from treatment facilities, and relates to the abuse of alcohol, medical drugs and illegal or 'street' drugs. These studies show that polydrug abuse is a common but varied phenomenon in different contexts. It poses special problems for therapy and social policy. Techniques of differentiating specific types of 'polytoxicomania' are outlined. It is concluded that future studies should attempt to distinguish clearly between such types, since, besides involving different substances, they pose distinct social problems and therapeutic challenges. International comparative studies would have great value only if they monitored both substance abuse and patterns of abuse. Such studies will necessitate the adoption of comparable methods and criteria.

## Introduction

It is generally assumed that 'polydrug abuse' or 'multiple drug abuse' plays an increasing role in the field of psychoactive drugs, and in particular, in relation to alcohol and illegal drugs. Even so, 'polydrug use' or 'misuse' are frequently undefined.

Although – with few exceptions – each single patient on the basis of the number of drugs consumed must be called polytoxicomanic (Nusselt 1980).

This is a fairly commonplace assertion, in which multiple drug abuse in a clinical setting is equated with dependence. A similar view has been advanced by Kielholz and Ladewig (1975):

In the past years we have increasingly observed the phenomenon of polytoxicomania so that in Switzerland today

60 per cent of the drug dependent people must be regarded as being polytoxicomanic.

In fact, heroin users who take other drugs may do so only occasionally or sporadically. It is not always clear whether abuse involves regularity, 'problems' or dependence. Under such conditions the more 'neutral' terms of 'multihabituation' or 'multiple drug abuse' may be more appropriate labels.

The term 'multihabituation' (Cohen and Ditman 1962) does not specify whether or not dependence is evident, while terms such as 'pan addiction' (Lingemann 1969) do imply such an assumption. Lingemann, for example, indicated that multiple drug use does involve dependence. In a number of earlier discussions of this phenomenon the term 'polytoxicomania' was used. This referred to multiple drug use without directly implicating physical or psychological dependence. Such discussions referred to the types of multiple drug use evident in many countries among young people in the 1960s, including the 'hippy' or 'flower child' period (Steinbrecher and Solms 1975, Janz 1975, Schmidbauer and von Scheidt 1981). There have also been attempts to differentiate between 'multiple abuse', and 'multiple dependence' (true 'polytoxicomania')(Klein, Boldt, Klein and Koppenhagen 1980). Keup (1983) distinguished between 'polyvalent abuse' and 'polytoxicomania', the latter involving dependence upon at least two substances.

Alcohol dependents who are also dependent upon medical drugs and illegal drug users who are also dependent upon alcohol and/or medical drugs represent the 'hard core' of multiple drug users. The treatment of such people has been more problematic than that of individuals who are dependent upon a single substance. Multiple drug dependence may be accompanied by severe withdrawal symptoms which may require intensive management. Accordingly, the future planning of treatment facilities will be assisted by studies into the extent and pattern of polydrug use and its related adverse consequences. There are many reasons for devising a more precise definition or definitions of 'polydrug abuse'.

At present no such clarity of definition exists. Some authors suggest that the occasional use of another opiate, such as codeine, by a regular heroin user constitutes 'polytoxicomania'. Others contend that such a label may only be applied to individuals who are clearly dependent upon substances from at least two distinctly different chemical groups. These views are clearly incompatible.

For the purpose of international comparison some form of agreed definition is needed, since local influences already introduce unavoidable differences in both results and their interpretation.

Very few studies of illegal drug use have related to more than a single country. Even so, illegal drug use is an international phenomenon. There are clear advantages to be derived if future epidemiological studies of drug use and misuse apply internationally comparable definitions and methods. The author has for some years attempted to develop a set of rules whereby polydrug abusers might be clearly described and specific subgroups distinguished.

## METHODS

The data to be described were produced by three long-term studies of the characteristics of patients with a history of substance abuse. The populations examined by these studies were as follows:

1. Newly-admitted patients to a 2000 bed psychiatric hospital over a nine-year period. Altogether 15371 (51.1 per cent) patients out of 30105 admissions had problems related to substance abuse (Keup 1985).

2. In the Substance Abuse Warning System (SAWS) of the Federal Republic of Germany the size of the main subgroups of drug abusers (alcohol, medical and illegal drugs) are predetermined by limiting each to approximately 300 people per year. Otherwise substance misusing patients are accepted at random by admission to hospitals for the treatment of their drug problems or other conditions.

The recording procedure used by the SAWS is illustrated by Table 12.1. This is elaborated below in relation to a study of 4410 people with drug-related problems. These were admitted to 25 institutions during the years 1976–9 and 1982–5.

3. 'DOSY' patients. These were approximately 10000 people with alcohol, medical and illegal drug-related problems who were admitted in 1982–3 to 50 institutions specializing in substance abuse.

### Instruments of Evaluation

1. *Psychiatric hospital survey.* As part of a continuing survey of all new admissions to a large psychiatric hospital, individuals were interviewed in order to determine which, if any, psychoactive drugs they had abused. They were then classified as indicated by Table 12.1. Each particular drug was not examined in detail, since

Table 12.1. The classification of clients under the substance abuse warning system

| Main Substance Group | Alone | In Addition | | | |
|---|---|---|---|---|---|
| | | Alcohol | Medical Drugs | Illegal Drugs | Both |
| Alcohol | 1 | XXX | | | |
| Medical drugs | 2 | | XXX | | |
| Illegal drugs | 3 | | | XXX | |
| | 1 | 2 | 3 | 4 | 5 |

*Note*: Each patient's drug use is indicated on this matrix by a single cross

this exercise was mainly concerned with a general classification to indicate the overall drug abuse career of respondents. This procedure was conducted as a guide for therapeutic responses. It is patient-oriented rather than drug-oriented.

2. *Substance abuse warning system (SAWS)*. SAWS (or *Früh-warnsystem zur Erfassung der Missbrauchsmuster chemischer Stoffe...*) was initiated in 1976 in order to create a continuing random access surveillance system whereby substance abuse could be monitored (Keup 1983). It was intended that this system would firstly assist decision making in relation to drug misuse and in the formulation of drug control policies and therapeutic responses in the Federal Republic of Germany. Secondly, it was also hoped that once the system was established and its utility demonstrated, it might serve as a basis for international comparisons if the involvement of other countries could be enlisted.

The institutions which participate in this scheme were selected to be representative of the whole country so far as was possible. This selection attempts to give due balance to criteria such as rural/urban, North/South, private/public, psychiatric university clinic/specialized addiction treatment units and areas with high/low rates of alcohol-related problems. Starting on January 1st each year all patients with drug-related problems who are admitted to SAWS institutions are interviewed. Each collaborating agency is allocated a quota of problem drinkers, medical and illegal drug abusers. These quotas are determined in relation to the previous year's admissions. A total of up to 900 addicts are interviewed each year of whom 100 are solely alcohol abusers, 200 have problems related to alcohol and medical and/or illegal drugs as well, 300 have problems involving prescribed drugs and 300 are abusers of illegal drugs.

Respondents are asked to provide information on all of the drugs that they have ever abused. Drugs used for medicinal purposes, unprescribed or prescribed, are not recorded unless such use appears to involve dependence. Thus a fairly comprehensive picture of each respondent's drug abuse career is reconstructed. The system is substance-oriented, whereas the second system, DOSY (see below) is patient-oriented. In relation to each drug, information is collected related to a number of topics. These include dosage, frequency and pattern of use, combination with other drugs, duration and intensity of use, experience of adverse consequences and the relative preference ('liking') for each drug in comparison with others. In addition, details are collected on each person's social and psychiatric history. Individuals are classified in relation to Figure 12.1 according to the substance that they mainly use and in relation to any other drugs used as well. Each group is classified for statistical purposes by the allocation of a two digit number. This indicates the appropriate line and column on the matrix illustrated by Table 12.1. These data are used to monitor changing trends in patient characteristics.

All data are evaluated by electronic data processing methods and compiled to yield profiles of drug abuse in general and of each substance for the year. These data are compared with those of the previous year. Changes occurring are brought to the attention of the authorities and are investigated in more depth and, if appropriate, by supplementary statistical instruments.

3. *Documentation system of the special hospitals for the treatment of substance abuse (DOSY)*. All patients admitted to some fifty treatment facilities for substance abuse are assessed by the use of an admission questionnaire. This collects information on basic details such as age, sex, religion and attitude towards religion, marital status and marital/partner relations, nationality, geographical location of residence, type of housing, education, employment and unemployment. In addition details are obtained on social status before and since drug use, previous treatment, duration of drug career, drug-related criminal activities and suicide attempts. Upon completion of in-patient therapy additional data are collected before patients are discharged. These include how the cost of treatment has been covered, which types of drugs

had been abused before treatment, symptoms at time of admission and their improvement by therapy, all diagnoses, length of treatment and type of release from hospital. Patients' progress after discharge is followed up one, two and four years later. All of the information collected is confidential and is safeguarded according to the rules of data protection.

The data elicited during treatment include details of polydrug use. These are collected using a more complex diagram (Table 12.5). This enables interviewers to classify patients in a more refined way. This makes it possible to distinguish between the main and additional substances of abuse and between dependent or non-dependent abuse. Altogether 36 subgroups may be distinguished using this procedure.

RESULTS

This chapter is confined to presenting a small part of the information obtained by these three studies. This review is primarily concerned with methodological issues. Accordingly emphasis is placed upon those aspects which directly relate to polydrug abuse, although a host of other information on these multiple drug abusers and other patients is collected by these studies.

1. Psychiatric Hospital Data

The pattern of polydrug use evident amongst patients included in this study is illustrated by Figure 12.1 (Keup 1985).

Individuals identified as substance abusers constituted 64.1 per cent of male and 32.0 per cent of female psychiatric patients at a hospital in a large urban area. Three-quarters of those identified as drug misusers were male. Amongst both sexes the largest subgroups were problem drinkers. The second largest subgroup of females was comprised of abusers of medical drugs. The corresponding male subgroup consisted of illegal drug users. Polydrug users represented 14.8 per cent of males and 21.8 per cent of females. The distribution of these subgroups is shown in Table 12.2.

In the alcohol/medical drug abuse group there is a large preponderance of female patients. In contrast there are more male patients in the alcohol/medical/illegal drug (AMI) group and, to a lesser degree, also in the AI and MI groups. This is due to the prevalence of illegal drug users in the male group.

This group of hospital patients is fairly representative of new admissions in other psychiatric hospitals, but the relevance of the

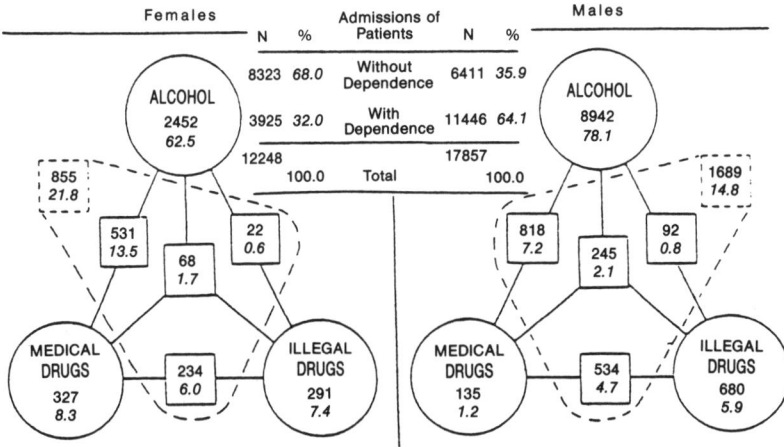

Figure 12.1. Patterns of polydrug abuse among psychiatric hospital patients 1976–84 (*after Keup, 1985*)

data as an indicator of patterns of drug abuse in the community at large is limited.

Table 12.2. Polydrug abuse among 15 371 patients with substance abuse newly admitted to a psychiatric hospital 1976–84

| Types of Drugs Abused | Females | | Males | | Total | |
|---|---|---|---|---|---|---|
| | Number | (%) | Number | (%) | Number | (%) |
| Alcohol/medical drugs | 531 | 62.1 | 818 | 48.5 | 1349 | 53.0 |
| Alcohol/illegal drugs | 22 | 2.6 | 92 | 5.4 | 114 | 4.5 |
| Medical/illegal drugs | 234 | 27.4 | 534 | 31.6 | 768 | 30.2 |
| Alcohol/medical/illegal drugs | 68 | 7.9 | 245 | 14.5 | 313 | 12.3 |

## 2. Substance Abuse Warning System (SAWS)

The distribution of patterns of drug use amongst 4410 patients investigated in the SAWS between 1976 and 1985 is shown in Table 12.3.

This system is designed to investigate all three major subgroups of drug abuse (alcohol, medical and illegal drugs). As noted above, the size of these three subgroups is arbitrarily set at 300 each per year, so that the relative size of the main substance

131

Table 12.3. Patterns of polydrug abuse among patients recorded by the substance Abuse Warning System 1976–85

| Main Substances | | Alone | A | P | I | Both | Polydrug abuse | Total |
|---|---|---|---|---|---|---|---|---|
| | | | | *Additional substances* | | | | |
| Alcohol | Number | 838 | XXX | 846 | 45 | 137 | 1028 | 1866 |
| (= A) | % | 44.9 | XXX | 45.3 | 2.4 | 7.4 | 55.1 | 42.3 |
| Medical drugs | Number | 843 | 347 | XXX | 43 | 35 | 425 | 1268 |
| (= P) | % | 66.5 | 27.3 | XXX | 3.4 | 2.8 | 33.5 | 28.8 |
| Illegal drugs | Number | 272 | 89 | 455 | XXX | 460 | 1004 | 1276 |
| (= I) | % | 21.33 | 7.0 | 35.7 | XXX | 36.0 | 78.7 | 28.9 |
| Total | Number | 1953 | 436 | 1301 | 88 | 632 | 2457 | 4410 |
| | % | 44.3 | | | 2457 | | 55.7 | 100.0 |

groups is not representative for the general population. This leaves untouched the horizontal percentage distribution in Table 12.3, i.e. within the groups. As this table shows, polydrug use was most commonplace amongst illegal drug users of whom 78.7 per cent had abused alcohol and/or medical drugs besides illegal drugs. Those least likely to have abused all three types of drugs were those in the medical drug group, of whom only 33.5 per cent had abused alcohol and/or illegal drugs.

The aim of SAWS is to obtain detailed information on the epidemiology of drugs of abuse rather than on those who abuse them. Even so, the relative frequency of different polydrug use combinations with the main subgroups is collected at random.

SAWS examines a sample of substance abusers admitted to treatment facilities, which means that these are people who may or may not be motivated to curtail or stop abusing drugs. It can be assumed that polydrug abuse in this group of motivated patients is more frequent than among abusers in the community.

### 3. Documentation System of the Special Hospitals for the Treatment of Substance Abuse (DOSY)

This system involves an assessment of all those admitted to agencies belonging to the Association of Treatment Facilities for Addicts (*Verband der Fachkrankenhäuser*) (Keup 1983, 1986). Approximately fifty such facilities admit over 5000 patients each year. Not every facility admits all types of drug abusers and both sexes.

Table 12.4. Subgroups of polydrug abuse dependence recorded under the documentation system of the special hospitals for the treatment of substance abuse (DOSY)

| *Simple polydrug abuse* | *Monopolar polydrug dependence* | |
|---|---|---|
| Simple, non-dependent abuse of all, but more than one substance(s) | Dependence on one of the additional substances plus simple abuse of the main substance(s) | |

| *Monopolar polydrug dependence* | *Bipolar polydrug dependence* | *Multipolar polydrug dependence* |
|---|---|---|
| Dependence upon main substance(s) plus simple abuse of additional substance(s) | Dependence on 2 substances of different main substance groups – with or without non-dependent abuse of other substance(s) | Dependence upon 3 or more substances – with or without non-dependent abuse of other substance(s) |

'Polytoxicomania'

DOSY employs a more detailed classification system than that illustrated by Table 12.1. Each section of that diagram is subdivided into four subsections. These differentiate between simple abuse and dependence in both dimensions. The subtypes are explained in Table 12.4

The pattern of simple drug abuse/dependence produced by the use of this system is shown in Table 12.5.

As this table shows, few of these patients were noted as being only non-dependent drug abusers. Presumably this is because these were 'problem drug users' who were in treatment facilities. A few individuals were not dependent on their 'main' substance, but upon additional drugs. For example, a chronic LSD user may be dependent upon a sedative, or a problem drinker may abuse or be dependent upon benzodiazepines. Most patients, however, are dependent upon their main drug of use and are also dependent upon a secnd drug. This seems typical for in-patients, but appears to be far less so for out-patients.

Treatment outcomes as well as substance abuse careers appear to vary for different subgroups of drug users, so that the inclusion in one of the groups allows a number of clinical conclusions to be drawn. The three main types of polydrug abuse are: (1) Simple

Table 12.5. In-patients admitted to special dependence clinics who were classified under the DOSY system (1982)

| Main Substance | | alone | Additional Substances | | | | | | | Total |
|---|---|---|---|---|---|---|---|---|---|---|
| | Abuse pattern | | Alcohol | | Medical drugs | | Illegal drugs | | Both substances | |
| | | | non-dependent | dependent | non-dependent | dependent | non-dependent | dependent | | |
| Alcohol | 1 non-dependent abuse | 73 | | | 8 | 2 | — | — | 1 | 84 |
| | 2 dependent abuse | 4108 | | | 312 | 268 | 32 | 23 | 78 | 4821 |
| Medical drugs | 3 non-dependent abuse | — | 1 | 1 | | | — | 1 | — | 3 |
| | 4 dependent abuse | 68 | 16 | 40 | | | 2 | 13 | 9 | 148 |
| Illegal drugs | 5 non-dependent abuse | 2 | — | — | — | 1 | | | — | 3 |
| | 6 dependent abuse | 135 | 12 | 21 | 3 | 33 | | | 41 | 245 |
| Total | | 4386 | 29 | 62 | 323 | 304 | 34 | 37 | 129 | 5304 |
| | | 0 | 1 | 2 | 3 | 4 | 5 | 6 | 7 | |

134

Table 12.6. In-patients admitted to special dependence clinics who were classified under the DOSY system (1982)

| Forms of polydrug abuse | Males Number | (%) | Females Number | (%) | Totals Number | (%) |
|---|---|---|---|---|---|---|
| *Without dependence* | | | | | | |
| Simple abuse of all substances | 3 | 0.5 | 7 | 2.0 | 10 | 1.1 |
| *Including dependence* | | | | | | |
| Monopolar polydrug abuse | 338 | 59.6 | 172 | 49.0 | 510 | 55.6 |
| Bipolar/multipolar polydrug abuse, 'polytoxicomania' | 226 | 39.9 | 172 | 49.0 | 398 | 43.3 |
| Totals | 567 | 100.0 | 351 | 100.0 | 918 | 100.0 |

polydrug use; (2) Monopolar polydrug dependence; (3) Bipolar/multipolar polydrug dependence. Table 12.6 shows the distribution of male and female patients between these categories.

As Table 12.6 shows, true 'polytoxicomania' was more commonplace amongst females than amongst males. The ratio females to males is quite variable among the different combinations of substances of the main groups ranging from 1:0.5 among the group of medical drug abuse with additional alcohol abuse (M–A) to the ratio of 1:4.3 in the group of illegal drug use with additional alcohol abuse (I–A). Between these ends of the scale the following ratios were found: 1:1.3 for the A–M group, 1:1.5 for I–M, 1:2.3 for M–I, 1:3.6 for A–I and 1:1.6 for all patients with polydrug abuse.

DOSY, as the two other recording systems presented above, related to persons with substance abuse; in the case of DOSY they are at least partly motivated to seek treatment. They thus do not represent the general addict population – which so far has hardly been reached in any study. It is difficult, although of great interest, to conduct surveys of substance use and abuse in the community. This is elaborated elsewhere in this book.

The respective distributions of different types of drug use noted by these three systems are depicted in Table 12.7 and 12.8.

## DISCUSSION

As Tables 12.7 and 12.8 show, the psychiatric hospital and the DOSY system produced similar results. Both employ random access procedures. In contrast SAWS emphasizes medical and illegal drug abuse, limiting for methodological reasons the

Table 12.7. Proportions of monodrug and polydrug misusers recorded by three treatment systems

| Type of institution | Total number of patients | Monodrug misuse | | Polydrug misuse | |
|---|---|---|---|---|---|
| | | Number | (%) | Number | (%) |
| Psychiatric Hospital | 15371 | 12827 | 83.4 | 2544 | 16.6 |
| Substance Abuse Warning System Institutions (SAWS) | 4410 | 1953 | 44.3 | 2457 | 55.7 |
| Clinics for Dependence Problems (DOSY) | 5304 | 4386 | 82.7 | 918 | 17.3 |

number of alcohol dependent persons included. Within the groups, however, SAWS also follows the rules of random access. SAWS results therefore deviate somewhat from the others. This highlights how important it is to define clearly in each study the sample from which results are drawn.

In all three systems alcohol/medical drug abuse was the most common combination. In the psychiatric hospital and SAWS the second largest subgroup related to medical/illegal drug use. In DOSY the second subgroup was that with abuse of alcohol, medical and illegal drugs. Earlier investigations (Keup 1985) have indicated that polydrug use in psychiatric hospital patients has increased since 1973 to a peak around 1976–8. Since then it has

Table 12.8. Relative frequency of different forms of polydrug misuse in three different treatment systems

| Type of institution | | Polydrug abuse | | | | |
|---|---|---|---|---|---|---|
| | | Alcohol/ medical drugs | Alcohol/ illegal drugs | Medical/ illegal drugs | Alcohol/ medical and illegal drugs | Totals |
| Psychiatric hospital | | | | | | |
| | N | 1349 | 114 | 768 | 313 | 2544 |
| | % | 53.0 | 4.5 | 30.2 | 12.3 | |
| Substance abuse | N | 1193 | 134 | 498 | 632 | 2547 |
| warning system | % | 48.5 | 5.5 | 20.3 | 25.7 | |
| institutions (SAWS) | | | | | | |
| Clinics for dependence | N | 648 | 88 | 53 | 129 | 918 |
| problems (DOSY) | % | 70.5 | 9.6 | 5.8 | 14.1 | |

slowly declined, reaching a plateau in 1980–1 which has subsequently been maintained. These changes appear mainly to have been due to a fall in polydrug abuse among illegal drug users and a larger decline among problem drinkers.

As shown above, methodological differences can influence the results of studies on polydrug abuse. But there also is a large number of local factors to be considered, influencing the aetiology, and through it the frequency, of polydrug abuse, as well as the kind of substances involved. Most important is the availability and the price of particular compounds, such as cocaine in present-day Europe, traditions in abuse patterns, the purity of the substances available, prescribed drug substitutes for illegal drugs. Many other factors can influence patterns of drug use and abuse.

Evidence from different countries suggests that personal motivations for substance abuse also have an important influence. Drug abusers who routinely try out new substances and new combinations – 'experimenters' – are particularly exposed to polydrug abuse. Even more predisposed to multiple drug abuse are those who may be called the 'omnivorous users' or 'gluttons' (Keup 1971, 1972), taking whatever drug they are offered. Whereas the former group often is rather resistant to dependence, the latter is not at all, being seriously exposed to frequent and life-threatening intoxication.

There are also some cases which are difficult to classify. In the course of a typical drug career, the dependent person usually gives up the substance well known to him or her only after having experienced a new substance well enough for such a decision. In between lies a time with abuse of both, either in an alternating or a concomitant abuse pattern. The eventual outcome of such practices may be a pattern of polydrug abuse.

*Cross tolerance* and cross dependence further confuse diagnosis and classification. Usually, the person who is dependent on heroin has developed tolerance not only to this substance but also to most other opiates and allied drugs such as methadone. Substituting methadone for heroin then requires large doses of the former but this often does not mean that the individual is dependent on methadone in the epidemiological/psychological meaning of the term. If he or she had a free choice and was offered both heroin and methadone, he or she undoubtedly would use heroin. If a drug user had used two opiates, he or she might successfully alternate the use of them and might slowly shift to the substance initially used as a substitute because of its pharmacological effects and safety. Cross dependence is, then, not a good measure for psychological dependence but is rather a pharmacological fact. The latter does not exclude psychological fixation. There also is a psychological tolerance to the effects of drugs developing, for example in relation to stimulants, leading, as with physiological tolerance, to dose increases. This process is particularly dangerous because physical tolerance provides at least a certain protection against overdose, but is missing in these cases. In the three studies described above, cross dependence is excluded unless psychological dependence justifies its inclusion. Only then is the situation judged to represent polydrug abuse.

An additional problem is the classification of a person abusing two particular substances of the *same group*, such as heroin and cocaine, or cocaine and cannabis. These are illegal drugs. Such abuse, of course, is polydrug abuse, and therefore should be classified accordingly. A similar problem arises with the sniffing of solvents and alcohol abuse, as well as with other such combinations. Each drug user should be registered under the most fitting category of polydrug abuse. No firm rules can be set and the decision in such cases rests with the informed judgment of an able and experienced investigator.

It is also a problem to distinguish between bipolar polydrug dependence and multiple changes from one substance abused in a dependent way to another which is also abused and upon which dependence develops. This can only be achieved by intimate knowledge of the entire substance abuse career – and a fully cooperative drug user!

Patterns of polydrug abuse are sometimes hard to classify. An example is the heroin user, who, if he or she can afford it and is in a mood to do so, adds cocaine intravenously to heroin to enhance the kick ('speedball'). Usually these individuals are not dependent on cocaine but easily slide into cocaine dependence when for some reason heroin becomes scarce. The opposite of this concomitant abuse pattern is the alternating or 'cycling' (Cohen 1981) abuse pattern of the amphetamine user who tries to calm down by the abuse of barbiturates, or of the barbiturate abuser who tries to get fit for work in the morning with the help of stimulants. Such a pattern can easily become routine. Then, a monopolar polydrug dependence can quickly change to a bipolar polydrug dependence.

To these examples the abuse of *alcohol* and *tobacco*, widespread in all three types of substance abusers, should actually be added, particularly in the alcohol dependent and opiate dependent. Caffeine is most often abused by individuals with alcohol problems.

## Conclusions and Recommendations

Polydrug abuse is usually a symptom of an advanced substance abuse career. Its existence, for this and other reasons, has serious implications for the health of the abuser as well as for public health. Polydrug abuse, therefore, must be included in the evaluation of drug problems.

If this is attempted, comparability with other samples, which might be compared across national borders, is only guaranteed if:

1. The sample investigated is described in all its essential details.

2. The local abuse situation in relation to the availability of single substances, degree of purity, price, local patterns of abuse as well as traditions, etc. are fully described.

3. The method used assures direct comparability between the results of the study and others, including those in other countries.

Three different clinical methods of classifying polydrug abuse have been described in this chapter. These are: (1) The Mental Hospital sample; (2) The SAWS sample; (3) The DOSY sample.

1. In the Mental Hospital sample, four groups of polydrug abuse, besides three types of monodrug abuse for alcohol, medical drugs and illegal drugs, were available for the classification of persons with substance abuse problems (Figure 12.1). Such a technique of classification is sufficient for the investigation of large samples by investigators who are not highly trained. This approach is relatively global and unsophisticated. It has limitations for the detailed planning of mental health facilities and other services. This system does not involve a differentiation between main and associated substances or between simple abuse and dependence (see below). An advantage of this system is that it refers to only seven subgroups, all of which are simple to understand.

2. The SAWS sample includes, as do the other two studies, data on alcohol, as modern studies should. It identifies 12 alternatives, three for monodrug and nine for polydrug abuse patterns. The coding diagram, in which each patient is identified with one cross in one box only, is shown in Table 12.1. The distinction between main substance and additional substance group has many advantages over Method 1. Most medical requirements for polydrug

studies related to individual and public health can be met satisfactorily. The precondition for classifying a patient in this way is a good knowledge of his or her individual abuse pattern and substance abuse career.

3. The DOSY sample uses the same criteria as the SAWS sample but offers an additional differentiation into simple abuse and dependence for the different groups (Table 12.5). Altogether 36 alternatives are available for classification, requiring large samples and assuring a sensible evaluation of the data. However, this classification requires a full knowledge of abuse questions as well as some pharmacological knowledge; it therefore cannot always be used. In the author's opinion, this approach has particular merit for research purposes.

The use of the classification system employed by SAWS (see para. 2, above), with the groups shown in Table 12.1, is recommended for all general purposes as well as for international comparison.

REFERENCES

Cohen, S. (1981) *Substance Abuse Problems*, pp. 91–2, New York: Haworth Press.

Cohen, S. and Ditman, K.S. (1962) Complications associated with lysergic acid diethylamide, *Journal of the American Medical Association* 181, 161.

Gerchow, J., Keup, W., Poser, W., Schrappe, O. and Ziegler, H. (1983) *Medikamenten-Abhängigheit*, pp. 44–6, Hamm: DHS.

Janz, H.W. (1975) Besondere Probleme der Psychotherapie bei Alkohol – und Drogenabhangigkeiten. In Steinbrecher, W. and Solms, H. (eds) *Sucht und Missbrauch* 2nd ed., vol. 6, pp. 95–116, Stuttgart: Thieme.

Keup, W. (1971) The typical 'Drug Career' and therapeutic approaches'. *Proceedings of 33rd Annual Meeting, Committee on Problems of Drug Dependency National Academy of Science*, II, 1049–1063.

Keup, W. (1972) Differences in therapy for drug users according to their motive for abuse. In Keup, W. (ed.) *Drug Abuse*, pp. 397–406, Springfield, Ill.: Thomas.

Keup, W. (1986) Dokumentations-System DOSY '82, Therapie-Daten der Stationären Behandlung für Suchtkranke (Sept. 1983); DOSY '83 (April 1986); DOSY '84 (Okt. 1986), *Verband der Fachkrankenhauser fur Suchtkranke*, Kassel.

Keup, W. (1983) Moglichkeiten zur Erfassung des Missbrauchsmusters von Medikamenten auf Bundesebene ('Frühwarn-System'). In Waldmann, H. (ed.) *Medikamenten-Abhangigkeit*, pp. 43–53, Wiesbaden: Akadem. Verlagsges.

Keup, W. (1985) *Zahlen zur Gefahrdung durch Drogen und Medikamente*. DHS-Informationsdienst 38, 1/2: 8–50.

Kielholz, P. and Ladewig, D. (1975) Erfahrungen in der Schwisez. In Steinbrecher, W. and Solms, H. (eds) *Sucht und Missbrauch*, vol. 8, pp. 91–112, Stuttgart.

Klein, K., Boldt, G., Klein, G. and Koppenhagen, A. (1980) *Taschenlexikon Drogen*, p. 158, Düsseldorf: Schwann.

Lingemann, R.R. (1969) *Drugs from A to Z*, p. 177. New York: McGraw-Hill.

Nusselt, L. (1980) Der soziale Niedergang des Süchtigen – Beeinflussung durch Art des Giftes, Missbrauchsmuster und Gesellschaftliche Einflüsse. In Keup, W. (ed) *Folgen der Sucht*, pp. 142–151, Stuttgart: Thieme.

Schmidbauer, W. and von Scheidt, J. (1981) *Handbuch der Rauschdrogen*, 6th ed., pp. 375, 490, 523. Munich: Nymphenburger.

Steinbrecher, W. and Solms, H. (1975) *Sucht und Missbrauch*, 2nd ed., vol. 1, pp. 44–5, Stuttgart: Thieme.

# 13. User Careers: Implications for Preventing Drug Misuse

WALTER WEISS

*Abstract.* This chapter presents a selective overview of the literature on changing patterns of drug use and drug misuse, with special reference to factors leading to initiation into and the cessation of such behaviour. It is noted that very often factors which foster drug use and misuse may also facilitate movement away from drug use or drug problems (remission). The identification of such influential factors is clearly important to the prevention of drug problems. A number of recommendations are advanced to improve research and policy related to the prevention of such problems.

## Introduction

Attempts to describe the careers of psychoactive substance users are based on two premises. Misuse of a psychoactive drug is first seen as an interaction process between the individual as the host and a drug as the agent. This process leads to progressively deeper involvement, due to the drug's addictive potential. Second, it is hypothesized that because of the particular psychopharmacological characteristics of a drug, and acquisition of tolerance, the course of dependence can be described as a career-like sequence of typical phases. Existing attempts at such career reconstruction usually refer to data (such as those in Chapter 12) from clinical populations, and therefore have some common limitations and implications.

The use and misuse of a substance are regarded as distinct behavioural patterns. Much of the practical concern of researchers relates to which factors relate to misuse or the experience of drug-related consequences. Such explanations necessarily deal with established drug problems, and thus may reflect a person's need to explain or excuse his or her deviance. The analysis of the process of dependence, if based on institutionalized drug users, may give little impression of the extent to which drug users in the community overcome their problems. As a consequence, drug dependence is sometimes regarded as a chronic state.

In contrast to this clinical approach, epidemiological data of non-institutionalized drug users, and the findings of recent longitudinal and experimental studies as well, give rise to a rather different view of drug use careers.

*Epidemiological data* on consumption patterns and the prevalence of problems related to the use of legal and illegal drugs show that a considerable number of people affected by drug problems never undergo formal treatment or become involved in legal procedures or other types of social responses.

There is growing evidence for the ability of some people to change their patterns of substance use in the direction of less problematic behaviour or to abandon drug use completely on their own: the occurrence of processes of so-called 'spontaneous remission' has been observed in *longitudinal studies* of abuse of different psychoactive substances (Stall and Biernacki, 1984). Fillmore (1985, 1987) found, through (meta-) analyses of longitudinal data on alcohol consumption patterns, that the incidence of problematic use and remission from it vary over life course as a function of age, sex and supposedly many more social and situational factors.

*Experimental studies* designed to investigate the concept of dependence by defining it on the basis of operational criteria, question the empirical validity of this concept. Experiments with alcohol dependent persons, for instance, showed that the alleged pharmacological effect of a moderate dose of alcohol to prime a craving for more can be mediated or even evoked by cognitive cues (Hodgson 1980; Stockwell, Hodgson, Rankin and Taylor 1982). Similar results were found in interviews with opiate users. Thus, Blackwell (1985) and Biernacki (1986) point out that notion and experience of 'craving' or 'loss of control' vary widely between individuals.

*Biographical data*, obtained in interviews with ex-addicts, revealed that patterns of use and misuse may sometimes hardly be distinguishable, even in the case of opiate use. Thus, subjects reported considerable individual differences in duration and intensity of consumption until symptoms of dependence became evident. Moreover, some respondents admitted that their cognitive orientation, namely, their conviction to keep consumption under control, played an important part in their relationship with drugs (Berger, Reuband and Widlitzek 1980). An analogous pattern has been observed by Blackwell. She describes a category of heroin users able to limit their opiate intake and to participate in a drug subculture over years without becoming fully committed to it. Conditions for this maintenance of a state of 'indefinite drift' (Blackwell 1983, p. 225) were tentatively located in a person's social environment and other individual characteristics.

This admittedly rough overview sheds light on the shortcomings of the 'clinical' career concept: besides the impact of addictive potential and psychopharmacological properties of drugs, the course of dependence proves to be influenced by social–psychological factors, and by the characteristics of salient situations and social interactions in the context in which drug consumption occurs. In the remainder of this chapter an attempt is made to provide an outline of a career concept which integrates and stresses those social–psychological components.

Whereas the 'clinical' approach to substance abuse careers seems suited to yield consequences with regard to appropriate therapeutical procedures, the proposed shift in perspective is mainly motivated by the practical interest in developing measures of (secondary) prevention. These related to preventing drug users or misusers developing severe or chronic problems.

LIFE COURSE USE OF DRUGS AND DRUG USE CAREERS

Initiation into the use of legal substances such as alcohol, nicotine and prescribed drugs, takes place early in life for most people in industrial societies. Through observation of current consumption patterns and participation in them, individuals learn about specific functions of a particular substance and how to use it in order to get particular effects and sensations. To the extent that the consumption of those drugs is an integrated element of a common life-style, people learn to use them in order to cope with specific (social) situations, inner states or somatic conditions. Thus, these lifelong processes of social transmission of knowledge and habits create a social or social-psychological dynamic complementary to the psycho-pharmacological dynamic of drug use.

The integration at least of legal drug use in our modern lifestyle has a twofold implication: first, there is exposure to drugs and drug use patterns which may vary with respect to intensity and type of drug as a function of age, sex and status roles held by the individual during life. Second, there is exposure to specific life situations which act as cues for the use of a drug. Such conditions vary markedly between individuals. Conversely, people often face the same or similar situations, tasks, difficulties and experiences during a particular period of life. It may, therefore, be concluded that conditions specific to life phases and experiences determine, in a relatively uniform manner, an individual's exposure to and relationship with drugs. The question then arises of how and to what extent such modal biographical constellations either contribute to the development of patterns of substance abuse or prevent it.

The concept of the life course use of drugs relates to a sequence of biographical stages which can trigger a change in an individual's drug use pattern. When changes occur, they are the result of the interaction between the characteristics of the drug and the social setting, and they can influence a person's drug use either in a synergic or competing way.

### Meaning and Patterns of Psychoactive Substance Use in Adolescence and Early Adulthood

Initiation into the use of legal drugs often starts early in life. In a recent study among schoolchildren in Switzerland 13 per cent of girls aged 11 to 12 reported use of non-prescribed drugs several times a month for headaches, and 5 per cent for nervousness and sleeplessness (Müller and Béroud 1987). In cultures which are permissive towards alcohol use young children already have a fairly good and realistic understanding of adults' drinking, its effects, symbolic meaning and so on (e.g. Jahoda and Cramond 1972, Aitken 1978, Penrose 1978, Weiss 1986). But whereas youth drinking has often been regarded and discussed in the perspective of imitating adults and of enacting adults' social role by using alcoholic beverages as significant attributes of that role, little attention has been paid to the fact that they develop their own meaning structures when drinking becomes peer group activity. Thus the attractiveness of alcoholic beverages may be based on different properties for young people than for adults. Even if drinking takes place on identical occasions such as social gatherings, underlying intentions and the significance attributed to it may vary widely.

Adolescents often judge adults' drinking to be ritualistic, a behavioural pattern that emphasizes the conventional forms of their conviviality and social interactions. Adolescents, however, seem to be more interested in intensifying social experiences by the use of alcohol. Moreover, these beverages prove to be very attractive as means to allow sensational experiences through producing altered mental states. As Eisenbach-Stangl (1986) points out, most of the adults' motives for drinking have little importance for (Austrian) adolescents and young adults, whereas they show higher preference to the stimulating and intoxicating effects of alcohol. The same tendency can be illustrated by interview data from children and adolescents in the French speaking part of Switzerland (Weiss 1986). Between the ages of 12 and 16 years, awareness of positive, mainly mood-changing, effects of alcohol increases remarkably, and about a quarter of adolescents report favourable attitudes to drunkenness and its effects.

Even young children are keenly aware of the fact that adults often drink alcoholic beverages in order to cope with all kinds of problems, sorrows, conflicts, pain and many more emotional states. But whereas they internalize in this way to manipulate subjective well-being, the application of that learning to themselves bears genuinely new forms. They are not satisfied with simply *managing* life, but in seeking happiness and self-actualization they use drugs to enhance experiences and to facilitate expressiveness (Stein-Hilbers 1985).

The predisposition of youth to expand and diversify the use of psychoactive substances can be interpreted as a reaction to their life experiences and as a corollary to basic needs. Alcohol or other drug uses are not always appropriate or even legal, but are often seen as a timely way of adaptation to the life conditions of young people; a way that is functional, since drug use meets vital needs. However, to the extent that this behavioural pattern splits up and turns out to be practised in an exclusively sub- or counter-cultural context, it is no longer a symbol of youthful lifestyle but becomes its central element. Psychoactive substance use then becomes a means to escape from restrictions and from the challenge they represent.

The relative ease of availability of drugs in youth subculture certainly helps to foster such a career development. Nevertheless, the crucial risk factor seems not to be availability but psychological orientation towards life. Biographical research by Berger and co-workers shows in fact that many opiate users did not need to be 'seduced' to use drugs but were anxious to do so (Berger *et al.* 1980). On the other hand, youth and early adulthood is a transitional life phase with relatively frequent occasions for life changes and other significant events. Therefore, both perception of the merits of an 'addicted lifestyle', and of the difficulties or chances to cope successfully with the challenges of life, may change over time. This kind of insight and experience is likely to be a trigger for remission of illicit drug use, a process which may sometimes be a disruptive lifestyle change. As Buchmann and Tecklenburg (1980) point out, to begin or to resume heavy drinking might be a sign and a means of ending a (more) deviant career.

## Psychoactive Substance Use In Adults

In many industrial countries, alcohol is the most popular and widely used psychoactive substance in the middle years of life. Cross-sectional data on drinking in Switzerland (Muller 1983) show on the one hand a decrease in the numbers of abstainers until about the age of 25, and an increase after 35; on the other hand, there is a very strong increase in men's average daily consumption until the mid-forties, and a slight decrease and stabilization afterwards. In contrast, women's average consumption is relatively low and stable throughout adult life. Since these data do not allow conclusions about life course use of alcohol, and the respective prevalence of alcohol abuse and problem drinking, reference is made to the findings of a review and meta-analysis of existing longitudinal research on alcohol use in the USA. These analyses show that the incidence of alcohol problems is highest in younger men but remission rates from these problems are also high. Whereas the incidence of heavy drinking and alcohol problems decreases with age, the probability of chronic drinking after the age of 40 increases, and the likelihood of chronicity for alcohol problems and social complications associated with alcohol use is highest in middle age (Fillmore 1987). These findings suggest that ageing processes, supposedly combined with decreased alcohol tolerance in later adulthood, lead to remission of problematic drinking patterns. These results also lend some support to the hypothesis that, due to other factors, events leading to changes in drug and alcohol use are likely to occur several times during life. The observed high remission rate among younger adults compared to the tendency for chronicity of heavy drinking and of alcohol problems in the middle years of life, casts doubt upon the concept of continuity of drinking problems. As Fillmore points out: 'We cannot assume that the drinking child is father to the drinking man' (Fillmore 1985b, p. 15). This raises the question of what the particular life circumstances and experiences in the middle years are, which prompt individuals either to develop chronic drinking patterns and problems or help them to avoid them.

The middle years of a person's life may represent a phase of relative stability in the private and occupational sphere. For most people, leeway for personal life choices and decisions becomes limited to the extent that they are assuming responsibility for a family. Furthermore, opportunities to make major job changes might become fewer too. This experience may often be accompanied by the insight that certain aspirations concerning occupational activities and/or material rewards are unlikely to be attained. Given this type of commonplace situation one may ask how individuals and social systems (i.e. families) adapt to these new and somewhat restricting life conditions, and what the potential contribution of drug use to this adaptation process could be.

Experimental studies indicate that expectancy states, due to cognitions about behavioural outcomes after drinking, are a relevant precondition for experiencing some of alcohol's effects (Room and Collins 1983). As a consequence, specific life experiences may not only cause different predispositions for alcohol consumption but specific susceptibility for particular effects attributed to it. In other words, individuals' drinking patterns might be influenced by their search for effects which fit into their habitual way of coping with reality. Substance use then becomes particularly rewarding, acting as an adjunct to a specific orientation towards life, and reinforcing the underlying developmental process.

Among the potential effects of (excessive) drinking, those leading to retreat from reality are best known. Yet influence in the opposite direction is as likely to occur but often is ignored. Thus drinking may facilitate everyday activities. The symbolic meaning of alcohol consumption and its socially desired effects may serve to assist creative problem solving or assist social interaction (Weiss 1985). If these effects are perceived as being functional, the individual and his or her social environment should be interested in maintaining them, thus reinforcing the corresponding drinking pattern. Problematic drinking patterns can be a temporary reaction to particular life circumstances, becoming obsolete when those circumstances or an individual's adaptation to them is changed.

148

## Similarities and Differences in Youth and Adult Substance Use

After this short review of general life conditions and psychoactive drug use from adolescence to middle age, attention is focused upon what these stages imply for the chronicity or cessation of problematic drug use.

1. It is a general characteristic of youth's social status that society is relatively tolerant of deviant behaviour by the young. Thus, young people may often experience intoxication and its sequelae without the risk of a major societal reaction, unless they commit very serious illegal acts. To the degree as such a behaviour is a means of protest, it can be expressed without prejudicial consequences.

2. Juvenile drug abuse is often a collective reaction to adverse and restrictive life conditions and occurs in the context of a group or youth subculture. On the contrary, adults' excessive drinking or misuse of non-prescribed drugs is an individual and often hidden coping strategy. This kind of deviance is not only less visible, but leads progressively to social isolation, and, as a consequence, to a lower chance of remission.

3. Remission for substance misuse may involve different rewards for young people and adults in the middle of life. Younger people may be more inclined than older people to use drugs to escape reality. In contrast, the constraints and frustrations of an adult's life, the perspective of 'becoming and being "ordinary"' (Biernacki 1986) implies a challenge and a chance to be successful. If, on the other hand, adult drug misuse is a means to cope with dissatisfaction, it has a primarily anaesthetic function. Consequently, the outcome of abstinence will be a rather painful confrontation with the person's actual life situation.

### UNDERSTANDING REMISSION FROM SUBSTANCE MISUSE

Compared to the large body of literature on remission in the perspective of the effectiveness of therapeutic interventions and the professional treatment system, research on spontaneous remission is sparse. This is largely due to the dominance of the 'disease concept' of addiction, and to the fact that most of our knowledge about the course of dependence and the recovery processes is based on clinical evidence. As a consequence, remission from an addiction career can hardly be conceived of as a quasi-natural recovery process managed by the drug dependent person. Only with the recent change in paradigms regarding dependence, is research interest in factors leading to and supporting spontaneous remission growing.

Probably one of the most important research findings in many of the available studies is that the reasons for starting a career as an opioid user also often help to end it. Youthful drug use may be an attempt to resist the limitations and constraints of adult life. An analogous situation arises for many users progressing in their careers when they face 'health problems, social sanctions, problems with significant others, and financial difficulties. The necessity of coping with such problems leads to the decision to stop misusing the substances in question, and thus to the building of "psychic change" or "motivation".' (Stall and Biernacki 1984, p. 17.) In a study on reasons for undergoing treatment, tiredness of the pressures associated with the lifestyle of illegal drug use and the need for change were judged significantly more important than extrapersonal factors such as availability of drugs and legal problems (Simpson 1986). As a consequence of the experience of the 'costs' of this lifestyle, those who undergo spontaneous remission may learn to live in this society, making certain mental reservations, thus regaining control over their lives.

Drug misuse remains a transitional phenomenon to the extent that it is a way for the user to become aware of his or her intrinsic values and to increase self-esteem through this experience. Thus, Blackwell describes as a characteristic common to those who achieve remission from drug use: 'Having experienced the psychophysiological event of dependence, they thought they understood how chronic opiate dependents felt about their drug use, but all could articulate reasons why they were different' (Blackwell 1985, p. 384). Claims to be able to control substance use, often considered as a manifestation of resistance to therapy, can be an important precondition for changing the pattern of a drug career.

If motivation and internal resources are necessary for change, they are not in themselves sufficient to evoke it. The expectations held by significant others are strong determinants of behaviour. Therefore, remission depends on the occurrence of a significant event which works in a double sense, as a trigger for personal change and as a signal, announcing and justifying this change to the person's associates. The fact that such events or 'significant accidents ... can even appear to be "strangely trivial" to the outside observer' (Stall and Biernacki 1984, p. 18), gives rise to the hypothesis that a person prepared to cease problematic drug use, at least unconsciously, may be seeking such a stimulus. Life events often mark the beginning of a new situation, providing new social relationships and opportunities to assume responsibilities.

Finally, stabilization of a new lifestyle goes along with the modification or redefinition of a person's self concept, and with the 'negotiation' of a new social identity within the context of significant others and reference groups. This task is often described as a lasting process, beginning with some kind of identity disruption and a tendency to move away from earlier life circumstances and experiences (e.g. Andersson, Nilsson and Tunving 1983). However, a remitter's self-acceptance, his or her perceived credibility and resistance against relapses will largely depend on an ability to integrate those stigmatizing experiences into the whole biography. This process may be facilitated if the person concerned becomes aware of why he or she had to go through this difficult phase and what has been learned by doing so.

### Preventing Substance Misuse – Some Suggestions

In the background of the preceding considerations, measures of *prevention* have to influence both the intensity of the exposure to drugs and to life experiences which foster drug use. If predisposition to drug use and misuse is a corollary of the habitual mode of coping with and adapting to reality, then research and intervention should focus on the interface between life experience and drug use.

For many people, the prospect of a continuous biographical development along the lines of occupational careers cannot be taken for granted. Individual lives vary considerably. But whereas learning at school pertains to competing successfully with others, almost no attention is paid to preparing people to overcome failure and dissatisfaction. Teaching and learning in this field may be even more important in adulthood, when the sense of controlling one's life gets lost: (a) Because a perspective of life changes and positive events is lacking; (b) Because of a lack of clear identity or stagnation of identity development; (c) Because of an extremely routinized course of everyday life.

Concrete measures may help people to build up a perspective and motivation for life changes, implying a modification of their attitudes to and patterns of substance use. Such changes might be fostered by:

1. Providing individuals with ideas for alternative rewarding activities and, correspondingly, getting them acquainted with new social settings.

2. Proposing and involving them in new identity-relevant experiences.

3. Helping them to vary daily routines and thus improving their subjective sense of control over life.

Some more specific measures, suited to prompt and facilitate a change of drug use could be adopted. These include the following:

*Promotion of a non-clinical view of remission* by disseminating the basic knowledge about 'natural' recovery processes and by changing attitudes, for instance, related to the significance of repeated relapse and ambivalent motivation for therapy.

*Provision of institutional structures in which health problems are treated* and where potential remitters can find support in a 'neutral' setting, where drug problems are not constantly emphasized.

*Routinely checking for health problems which may be due to substance abuse.* Confront concerned persons with the diagnosis and refer them to a drug counsellor or other appropriate service.

*Improving awareness of possible ways whereby people might refrain from or avoid substance abuse.* This can be done through teaching all personnel working in the health care system and allied institutions about possible methods of encouraging drug abusers to adopt new lifestyles.

As a rule it is suggested that preventive interventions will be more promising if they envisage a general change in orientation towards life rather than the mere modification of substance use habits. Instead of being an aim in itself, a change of drug use patterns should assume symbolic value, indicative of a basic change in lifestyle.

### Monitoring Dependence Problems and Progress in Their Prevention

It is difficult to evaluate prevention approaches which stimulate and foster recovery from problematic drug use outside drug treatment institutions. However, two procedures seem fairly well suited to provide the necessary empirical data for these purposes, and are recommended for both national use and international comparisons:

1. Periodic screening tests for specific population groups, involving detailed measures of physiological and psychological indicators of substance use and related (health) problems. Researchers should make additional data available, particularly on the

overall socio-economic situation at the time of the study, adequacy of health care and social services, characteristics of the informal supportive structure of that context (for example the existence of self-help groups).

2. Longitudinal studies on developmental patterns of substance use and its associated problems, combined with self-reported data on perceived life conditions, individual life experiences, anticipation of problems and positive events in the future of both occupational and private life. Such studies should be designed in a quasi-experimental way, with varying frequencies and intensity of data collection, in order to control panel effects. Also, nonresponse and attrition should be reduced by providing special incentives for co-operating with such studies.

All research in this general area should provide proper safeguards to protect those covered by such studies from any adverse consequences. Thus, protection should be made explicit and should be explained in a comprehensible way to all of those co-operating with such research.

REFERENCES

Aitken, P.P. (1978) *Ten-to-Fourteen-Year-olds and Alcohol*, Edinburgh: HMSO.
Andersson, B., Nilsson, K. and Tunving, K. (1983) Drug careers in perspective, *Acta Psychiatrica Scandinavica* 67, 249–57.
Berger, H., Reuband, K-H. and Widlitzek, U. (1980) *'Wege in die Heroinabhangigkeit', Zur Entwicklung abweichender Karrieren*, München: Juventa.
Biernacki, P. (1984) *Pathways from Heroin Addiction. Recovery Without Treatment*, Philadelphia: Temple University Press.
Blackwell, J.S. (1983) Drifting, controlling and overcoming: Opiate users who avoid becoming chronically dependent, *Journal of Drug Issues* 12, 2, 219–35.
Blackwell, J.S. (1985) Opiate dependence as a psychophysical event: Users' reports of subjective experiences, *Contemporary Drug Problems* 12, 3, 331–50.
Buchmann, M. and Tecklenburg, U. (1980) *Deviante Karrieren Jugendlicher, Alkoholmissbrauch und der Einfluss Korrektiver Interventionen*, Bericht Teil 1 an den Schweiz. Nationalfonds. Zurich/Lausanne, Soz. Institut der Universität/Schweiz. Fachstelle für Alkoholprobleme.
Eisenbach-Stangl, I. (1986) Die Lehrjahre des Trinkens. Trinkmuster von Jugendlichen in Oesterreich, *Drogalkohol* 10, 1, 3–21.
Fillmore, K.M. (1985a) Prevalence, incidence and chronicity of drinking patterns and problems among men as a function of age: A longitudinal and cohort analysis, *British Journal of Addiction* 82, 77–84.
Fillmore, K.M. (1985b) A meta-analysis of the epidemiological results of existing alcohol-related longitudinal studies by age and sex: Implications for the intervention and prevention of alcohol problems. *Paper presented at the 34th International Congress on Alcoholism and Drug Dependence*, Calgary: ICAA.

Hodgson, R.J. (1980) Degrees of dependence and their significance. In Sandler, M. (ed.) *Psychopharmacology of Alcohol*, pp. 171–7, New York: Raven.

Jahoda, G. and Cramond, J. (1972) *Children and Alcohol*, London: HMSO.

Müller, R. (1983) *Trinksitten im Wandel*. Arbeitsberichte der Forschungsabteilung, Nr. 13. Lausanne (Schweiz. Fachstelle für Alkoholprobleme).

Müller, R. and Béroud, G. (1987) *La Santé – Pour les Adolescents Problème?* Rapport no. 16 du dept. de recherche. Lausanne: Institut Suisse de Prophylaxie de l'Alcoolisme.

Penrose, G.B. (1978) *Perceptions of 5- and 6-Year-Old Children Concerning Cultural Drinking Norms*. Unpublished PhD Thesis, Berkeley: University of California.

Room, R. and Collins, G. (1983) *Alcohol and Disinhibition: Nature and Meaning of the Link*, Research monograph 12, Rockville: U.S. Department of Health and Human Services.

Simpson, D.D. (1986) Addiction careers: Etiology, treatment, and 12-year follow-up outcomes, *Journal of Drug Issues* 16, 1, 107–22.

Stall, R. and Biernacki, P. (1984) Spontaneous remission from the problematic use of substances: An inductive model derived from a comparative analysis of the alcohol, opiate, tobacco and food/obesity literatures, *International Journal of the Addictions* 21, 1–23.

Stein-Hilbers, M. (1985) Selbstreflexive Ansatze in der Drogenforschung, *Psychologie und Gessellschaftskritik* 9, 3, 95–106.

Stockwell, T.R., Hodgson, R.J., Rankin, H.J. and Taylor, C. (1982) Alcohol dependence, beliefs and the priming effect, *Behaviour Research Theory and Therapy* 20, 513–22.

Weiss, W. (1985) Learning about uses of alcohol in a wet culture, *The Drinking and Drug Practices Survey* 20, 3–6.

Weiss, W. (1986) *Soziale Representätionen bei Kindern und Jugendlichen*, Arbeitsbericht der Forschungsabteilung, Nr. 15, Lausanne: Schweiz. Fachstelle fur Alkoholproblem.

# 14. Substance Abuse Careers: Attempts to Quantify the Course of Dependence

WOLFRAM KEUP

Attempts to identify the typical features of alcohol dependence were pioneered by Jellinek (1942, 1952). This authority described 'alpha–/gamma' and 'beta–/delta alcoholism' and the course of alcohol dependence. The latter involved prodromal, critical and chronic phases together with that of rehabilitation. Although Jellinek's typologies are still extensively used in treatment programmes they pose a number of serious scientific problems due to incongruities in symptomatology. Attempts have been made to classify other forms of drug dependence, notably those relating to medical and illicit (street) drugs. Keup (1971, 1972a) delineated a 'career model' of five strata. Vaillant (1973, 1983) has provided a valuable description of the careers of illicit drug users as well as a parallel description related to people with alcohol problems. Detailed descriptions of opiate use careers have been produced by Maddux and Desmond (1981) and on alcohol dependence and alcohol use by Plant (1979), Heather and Robertson (1981), Thorley (1981), Edwards (1984), Haver (1987) and many others.

Edwards (1984) stressed the differences between individual 'careers' and the 'natural history' or typical career of alcoholism. However, such a distinction is not the concern of this brief review which is focused on the methodology whereby the course of dependence might be examined.

As already noted in Chapter 5, none of the proposed typologies has been widely accepted. In addition, an extensive body of good longitudinal data on defined drug careers does not yet exist. One of the main reasons for this paucity of information is the complexity generated by the involvement of a large variety of chemical compounds, and the many combinations of temporal sequences by which they may be abused.

155

Nevertheless, many drug dependent people exhibit fairly uniform drug taking histories. This topic, however, still warrants further detailed research.

1. It would be of great value if typical drug careers could be isolated from the spectrum of symptoms. This would necessitate describing symptoms and their course. Randomly selected samples of medical drug, illicit drug and alcohol users would need to be assessed in relation to the frequency and course with which specific symptoms occur. Thus, such 'typical' careers might be delineated.

2. Clinically, it is evident that individuals who are dependent upon several drugs may be more difficult to treat than those whose dependence is related to a single drug. This has been elaborated in Chapter 12. In addition, the duration of a substance abuse career is also of prognostic interest, with the early and late phases being more favourable than the chronic phase. This, however, varies in relation to the psychopharmacological profiles of the drug being abused.

3. The relapse rate is also different amongst various career types of drug users. Accordingly user careers are highly relevant to the assessment of prognosis.

4. The type of treatment best suited to the management of some drug users at specific points in their user careers appears, from clinical experience, to be different. Very little firm evidence has been collected in relation to this important matter. This lack of information is rather surprising, since it could be expected that such criteria would be of considerable value in the choice of appropriate treatment approaches for individuals with drug problems.

The early 'domino' or 'escalation' theory of the course of drug abuse has proved to be an over-simplification (Keup 1972a). Even so, some drug users do appear to move from one type of drug use to another (e.g. Keup 1972b, Kandel 1982).

'Substance abuse' is used here to cover the abuse of alcohol, tobacco, medical and illicit (street) drugs. The careers of substance abusers need to be examined with reference to the following key factors:

A. As noted in Chapter 13, a large body of evidence has been accumulated on why and how people enter a drug career, yet less is known about why and how people achieve remission or cease drug use. In addition to those who die in the course of their careers and those who are successfully treated, there is a large number of persons who manage to stop or curtail drug use unaided, with little or no 'professional' help. Very little is known about details of mechanisms and the course of such 'spontaneous remissions'. This is regrettable, because such remission may have important therapeutic implications.

B. Relapse into substance abuse after treatment or after a spontaneous drug-free period is not always synonymous with the reinstatement of full dependence or addiction. A number of relapses, and the experience gained from such episodes, clearly help some people to obtain the final motivation for ceasing drug abuse. Relapse, in many cases, is part of a user career.

C. The final form of a user career is rarely indicative of an individual's complete user career. There are, for example, three commonplace types of cocaine user: (1) The young executive, who begins to use cocaine largely to the exclusion of other drugs; (2) Heroin users, who use cocaine before and after opiate initiation, with cocaine initially acting to accentuate the 'flash', 'rush' or other effects of heroin; (3) Cannabis users, who, having been described as 'pseudo jet set people', seek stronger euphoric effects after a period of marihuana or hashish use. Differences in drug history are of great importance to the management of an individual during therapy.

D. Drug careers have changed over time. Political ideologies, the 'flower children', serenity and peace and many other factors, all had an impact on the formation and evolution of user careers. This must be considered carefully when the career is analyzed together with the patient in conversation related to recollection of the beginnings of drug problems. Most contemporary users are quite remote from the romanticism of the 1960s and 1970s. User careers have become shorter, harder and more involved with crime.

E. User careers do not only involve drugs. Even so, the involvement of particular substances in the progress of a career and the concomitant use of more than one drug at any time are of great importance. Many social factors, such as public acceptance, legal issues and the availability of treatment alternatives, may exert major influences on user careers. It is often not fully appreciated to what extent a user career may have positive psychological aspects. The drug scene often confers social status, and such rewards may have a big influence on the drug user and upon treatment prognosis. These, and other social factors, are major influences upon, or obstacles to, effective treatment.

F. Atypical careers may be evident when drug dependence is secondary to another primary psychiatric condition. Such atypical careers vary widely and often have bizarre features if related, for example, to schizophrenia or mental subnormality. Such patients have to be treated differently from other drug abusers, with priority accorded to management of the primary psychiatric condition.

## Summary

The differentiation of substance abuse by type, drugs involved, severity of dependence, duration and stage of career, permits a quantification of most user careers. Such quantification depends, of course, upon the application of uniform criteria and procedures which are not elaborated in this commentary due to lack of space. Much scientific work is required to delineate such career characteristics, so that comparable and reproducible recording procedures may be adopted in different countries in order to produce comparable information. Those who seek to conduct such comparative epidemiological studies should attempt to describe user careers with the highest degree of precision. Such workers should be encouraged to develop widely and internationally acceptable criteria and methods.

The magnitude of the problem of drug abuse can be properly assessed through quantification, not only of the number of abusers, but also by assessment of the severity of dependence. The use of a common terminology and standard descriptions of substance abuse careers are indispensable if one hopes to compare levels of drug abuse in different countries.

REFERENCES

Edwards, G. (1984) Drinking in longitudinal perspective: Career and natural history, *British Journal of Addiction* 79, 175–83.

Haver, B. (1987) Drinking habits of female alcoholics 3–10 years after treatment, *Acta Psychiatrica Scandanavica* 75, 397–404.

Heather, N. and Robertson, I. (1981) *Controlled Drinking*, London: Methuen.

Jellinek, E.M. (1942) *Alcohol Addiction and Chronic Alcoholism*, New Haven, Conn.: Yale University Press.

Jellinek, E.M. (1952) Phases of alcohol addiction, *Quarterly Journal of Studies on Alcohol* 13, 673–84.

Kandel, D.B. (1982) Epidemiological and psychosocial perspectives on adolescent drug use, *Journal of the American Academy of Child Psychiatry* 21, 328–47.

Keup, W. (1971) The typical 'drug career' and other therapeutic approaches, *Proceedings of the 33rd Annual Meeting of the Committee on Problems of Drug Dependence*, National Research Council,

National Academy of Science, Toronto, 11, 1049, 1063.

Keup, W. (1972a) Aktuelle Probleme des Rauschmittelmissbrauches in New York unter besonderer Beruecksichtigung der 'Domino-Theorie'. In Ehrhardt, H.E. (ed.) Perspektiven der heutigen Psychiatrie, pp. 141–51, Frankfurt: Gerhards.

Keup, W. (1972b) Differences in the therapy for drug users according to their motive for abuse. In Keup, W. (ed) *Drug Abuse – Current Concepts of Research*, pp. 397–406, Springfield, Illinois: Thomas.

Maddux, J.F. and Desmond, D.D. (1981) *Careers of Opioid Users*, New York: Praeger.

Plant, M.A. (1979) *Drinking Careers: Occupations, Drinking Habits and Drinking Problems*, London: Tavistock.

Thorley, A. (1981) Longitudinal studies of drug dependence. In Edwards, G. and Busch, C. (eds) *Drug Problems in Britain*, pp. 117–170, London: Academic Press.

Vaillant, G. (1973) A 20-year follow-up of New York narcotic addicts, *Archives of General Psychiatry* 29, 237–41.

Vaillant, G. (1983) *The Natural History of Alcoholism*, Cambridge, Mass.: Harvard University Press.

# 15. Constraints upon Policy

MARTIN PLANT

*Abstract.* Policies to curb the use and misuse of psychoactive drugs are constrained by many factors. These may be dichotomised into competing demands upon resources and factors which foster drug use and misuse. This review outlines some of the complex aetiological theories which have been advanced to explain drug-related behaviour. The implications of these theories for public policy are discussed. It is concluded that some aetiological factors are probably intractable, and that only some environmental influences may be countered. The constraints upon demand reduction, availability curtailment and the provision of help for problem drug users are briefly discussed.

## Introduction

Social policy in relation to psychoactive drug use and misuse is influenced by a multiplicity of competing and often inhibiting factors. This chapter sets out to identify and to discuss some of these. It is hoped that in so doing drug policies will be set in a realistic context in relation to what they may practically achieve. A fundamental issue in implementing policies to regulate drug use and to prevent or minimise drug-related harm is the fact that both drug use and misuse are fostered by a variety of factors, some of which are powerful and which may be intractable. Accordingly, this review begins with a brief outline of aetiological theories related to both 'normal' and 'problematic' or 'harmful' patterns of psychoactive drug use. Thereafter, the relevance of these factors is discussed to the facilitation or obstruction of policy.

### AETIOLOGY OF DRUG USE AND MISUSE

A wide range of theories have at various times been advanced to account for the use and misuse of alcohol, tobacco, illegal and prescribed drugs. Several general reviews have been produced in recent years (Fazey 1977, Plant 1981a, Peck 1982). These have concluded that drug use and misuse are caused by many factors acting both singly and in combination.

The main implication of the complex aetiology of drug use and misuse is that no single theory can explain them and no single policy is likely to control use or prevent misuse.

The effects of any drug depend upon an interaction between the substance used, the characteristics of the user and the environment in which use occurs. The main factors which have been highlighted as contributing to drug use and to drug-related problems may be subdivided into constitutional, individual and environmental.

### Constitutional (or Biological) Factors

Constitutional theories are concerned with either biological predispositions or with the relationship between the drug and the body. It has been suggested that depressant drugs, such as alcohol, benzodiazepines and opiates, might appeal to people in need of relaxation. Conversely, stimulants such as amphetamines and cocaine, might attract extroverts. Animal studies have indicated that there sometimes does exist a genetic predisposition to use specific drugs. There is a growing body of evidence that inherited factors in humans may predispose people, for example, to experience alcohol-related problems (Peck 1982).

### Individual Factors

Individual theories are largely concerned with either unusual personality traits, or more general factors, such as introversion and extroversion. These have variously been linked to the use of drugs and the development of dependence or drug-related problems.

It is a commonplace belief that there is a distinctive type of personality that is particularly likely to develop drug problems. Clinicians have frequently noted that immaturity, dependence and other characteristics are common amongst those with severe alcohol and drug problems (e.g. Kessel and Walton 1965). In fact, such observations may relate more to the consequences of drug problems than to their causes. Available evidence does not suggest that there is a distinctive type of personality that is especially likely to develop drug problems. Existing studies have produced highly varied and conflicting results. They indicate that institutionalised drug users (for example those in clinics) may often be rather atypical in relation to various psychological constructs. Even so, such people do not appear to differ either from other institutionalised individuals, or even from the general population of the same age, sex and social background. Most drug users are unremarkable in relation to their general intelligence.

Individuals recorded by official agencies as problem drug users often have histories of psychiatric illness combined very often with stressful life events. In general, such disturbance or other types of 'deviance' are most evident in relation to users of substances which are illegal and used only by a small minority of the population. If a drug is both legal and widely used, its users and misusers are accordingly far less unusual. Again the evidence varies considerably. Some studies have concluded that a high proportion of institutionalised problem drug users have histories of prior psychiatric disturbance. Others disagree.

Males are generally far more likely than females to use psycho-active drugs, with the exception of prescribed drugs such as tranquillisers. To a large extent cultural factors may explain this difference. In some countries drug use amongst females has increased during recent years and in association drug problems amongst women have also proliferated. Males are generally far more likely than females to infringe the law. This could partly explain why females are less likely than males to use illegal drugs such as opiates. Biological factors certainly have some impact. As already noted the sexes differ in relation to their reactions to specific drug doses. Males are also more aggressive than females. This too may influence illegal or socially disapproved forms of drug-related behaviour (e.g. Collins 1981, Brain 1986).

In some countries, young people, notably those in their teens and twenties, are especially likely to use drugs or to experience drug-related accidents, such as those on the roads, or drownings. The age profile of drug users varies markedly between different countries even though illegal drugs use appears generally most common amongst young males.

It has been suggested that some people use drugs as a form of self-medication, that drug use is prompted by hedonism, a basic human need for altered states of consciousness (Weil 1972), from curiosity, as a form of self-destruction, risk-taking, or to resolve personal problems.

### Environmental Factors

Environmental factors include social, cultural, economic, political and historical influences.

*1. Family disturbance.* Much attention has been paid to the family background of drug users, especially those who come to the attention of 'official agencies' due to drug-related problems. Many studies have concluded that such institutionalised drug users have come from disturbed or abnormal backgrounds. Broken homes and early experience of heavy alcohol and drug use by parents are commonly reported by such individuals. The alleged link between such disturbance and drug use becomes less apparent when control groups of other people have been examined in comparison. Surveys provide ample evidence that the majority of casual or 'normal' drug use does not involve people from broken homes. However, a number of studies have indicated that indeed heavy or problematic users of drugs are significantly more commonplace amongst those who do come from disturbed homes.

*2. Educational and work problems.* There is abundant and convincing evidence that many institutionalised young drug users exhibit signs of educational disturbance, notably truancy. Older drug users, including problem drinkers, sometimes experience work difficulties, but it is difficult to ascertain if these were due to drug misuse or whether both the drug misuse and the work problems were caused by other factors.

Drug use and misuse occur amongst all strata of society. Even so, different subgroups have characteristic styles and fashions of drug use. There is little doubt that some forms of drug problem are more prevalent amongst some social groups than others. For example, in the United Kingdom and in the United States, tobacco smoking and therefore tobacco-related diseases are more commonplace amongst manual than amongst non-manual workers (Royal College of Physicians 1983). It is emphasised that drug use and misuse in various guises occur against all social groups, even though both patterns of use and types of problem may vary considerably. There is evidence that illegal drug use is sometimes associated with unemployment (Smith 1987).

One of the most commonly noted reasons for drug use is peer pressure to experiment or to join in social drug taking. A number of studies of young people have drawn attention to the role of such pressure in encouraging individuals to begin to use both legal and illegal drugs (Davies and Stacey 1972, Plant 1987).

Some types of drug use are symbolic in different contexts. Many young people use legal and illegal drugs as tokens of maturity or rebellion. Frequently such substances are used as facets of sociability, sophistication or hospitality. Religion and ideology may exert strong influences upon the use or non-use of specific drugs. This is exemplified by the Islamic proscription of alcohol, or the avoidance of both alcohol and tobacco by groups such as the Amish in the United States.

People in different occupations vary significantly in relation to their drinking and smoking habits, and in relation to the use and avoidance of other substances. Many reasons account for such differences. These include job stresses, traditions, access to alcohol at work, freedom from supervision and the possibility that some jobs may attract people who are predisposed to develop alcohol or other drug problems (Hore and Plant 1980).

One of the most important factors linked to use and misuse is the availability of drugs. This involves the price, distribution and marketing of both legal and illegal substances. Availability is a key factor in relation to implementing policies to curb drug misuse. This is elaborated below.

*Other factors*. Innumerable general factors have been suggested as contributing to drug use and misuse. These include alienation or 'anomie', unemployment, affluence (Young 1971, Goode 1972, Smith 1987) and the availability or scarcity of alternative substances or gratifications (Weil 1972, Gossop 1987).

### THE IMPLICATIONS OF AETIOLOGY FOR POLICY

Drug use and misuse are influenced by many different factors. Some of these, such as curiosity and peer pressure, may foster initial or 'normal' drug use, such as social drinking in countries in which alcohol is legal, or the use of illicit substances such as cannabis and opiates which are proscribed in most countries. Other factors, such as family backgrounds and stressful life events, may foster heavy drug use and drug dependence. Aetiology has central relevance to social policy, since it implies that any attempts to discourage or to restrict certain forms of drug-related behaviour (such as drunken driving or heroin use) have to operate in conflict with other factors which may be very powerful indeed.

MARTIN PLANT

Some aetiological factors are either intractable or are very difficult to counter. These include constitutional predispositions and individual traits. It may not be possible to change people's biological and psychological make-up. Even so, it is worth identifying subgroups which are, in some respects, 'at risk' for reasons of their ethnicity, age, sex, physiology or background. Indeed, a considerable amount of epidemiological work has been undertaken to identify such high-risk groups. The latter are clearly a key focus for efforts to prevent drug problems or to support those who have already developed such problems (e.g. Cahalan and Room 1974, Kandell 1982). It is important to emphasise that, since patterns of drug use vary considerably amongst different subgroups, so many policy initiatives need to be specifically oriented to particular subgroups with singular characteristics, problems and needs.

Other aetiological factors are more worthwhile targets for attack by social policy. These are all environmental. As already noted, possibly the most obvious of these factors is the availability of drugs. Other potentially fruitful targets for policy are ideologies and peer pressure to use drugs.

### OPTIONS FOR POLICY

Policies to prevent the misuse of drugs may be designed to restrain demand or to restrict supply. In addition, there is a clear need to provide help and support for those who are harmed directly or indirectly by drug misuse. The latter include not only those who are excessive or inappropriate drug users, but also their families and associates, or the victims, for example, of drunken driving or drug-related crime.

Perhaps the ideal solution of drug misuse would be the reduction of the demand for some drugs and elimination of the demand of others. In most countries drugs such as heroin are illegal, and social policy is geared towards eradicating or at least penalising the use of such drugs. In many countries alcohol and tobacco are used quite widely, and this use is supported by powerful legal vested interests and is buttressed by expensive advertising (Levine and Lilienfield 1987). The health evidence against tobacco is overwhelming and incontrovertible. Accordingly, reasonable health policy is to attempt to dissuade people from smoking at all (Royal College of Physicians 1983). In contrast, official policy in most countries is not to discourage drinking but to minimise alcohol-related harm. In some countries, such as Finland or the

165

Netherlands, public policy also seeks to reduce alcohol consumption or to discourage alcohol use. The existence of these differing objectives and legal positions creates a confusing and rather inequitable basis upon which to build a rational set of preventive policies. Health education is a popular and widely esteemed approach, whereby it is hoped that the demand for drugs may be curbed. Ideally, people should be provided with accurate information about the potential dangers of drugs, and would thereafter avoid them or use them in moderation and safety. Sadly, humans are not wholly rational, and, as already indicated, drug use is motivated and fostered by many influences. It is a problem both for health education and for drug policy in general that *health* is only one of several relevant issues affecting drug control policies. It is, for instance, difficult to explain to children why, if tobacco inflicts such a horrific toll of morbidity and mortality, it is legally available.

Health education ventures related to drugs have generally produced rather disappointing and sometimes negative results. Kalb (1975) lamented that there was almost no credible proof that alcohol education had influenced the drinking habits of those who had been exposed to it. Kinder, Pape and Walfish (1980) concluded that drug and alcohol education programmes had indeed been overwhelmingly unsuccessful in relation to changing behaviour. In addition, they concluded that amongst student populations such programmes 'may exacerbate the use of drugs and alcohol'. Schaps, Dibartolo, Moskowicz, Bailey and Churgin (1981) and Bandy and President (1983) reached similar conclusions. These disappointing findings may be partly explained by evidence suggesting that the more young people know about drugs, the safer they perceive them as being (Glaser and Snow 1969, Swisher 1971). In both the UK and USA tobacco use has declined substantially during recent years. It is therefore rather surprising to discover that Thompson (1978), reviewing English language reports on tobacco education between 1960 and 1976, concluded that most appeared to have had little effect. An equally cautious assessment has been reached by the (British) Royal College of Physicians (1983). There is, it must be noted, some rather more reassuring evidence (e.g. Gillies and Willcox 1984). Even so, it is clear that health education has probably not yet produced impressive results, certainly in relation to alcohol and illegal drugs. Education is, and will continue to be, an important arm of drug policy. It can only be regarded as experimental, and should not be conducted on the basis of unrealistic expectations of what it may achieve. Ultimately health education is unlikely to be a solution for drug problems. Peer pressures and curiosity are sometimes extremely compelling and some, even potentially dangerous drugs, do have enjoyable effects. Educational messages have to compete with counter information which may be far more pervasive, better organised and also long established or deeply entrenched. A number of 'anti-drug' campaigns have been conducted which present a wholly negative image of drug use. Such campaigns are often staged for political rather than educational reasons, and although the attractions of such ventures are obvious (being a highly visible affirmation of concern), they appear to have little, if any, desirable impact upon drug use behaviour.

As noted by Smart (1979) there are some encouraging signs. Educational campaigns seem most effective when linked to the increased application of a law, for example, related to drunken driving. As concluded by Ross (1984) the effectiveness of such laws does appear to depend upon public perception of the likelihood that offenders will be apprehended and convicted.

There is a clear link between the availability of a drug and the level of problems associated with it. In consequence, the minimisation of drug misuse must inevitably rely to a large extent upon curbing availability of psychoactive substances. Two major problems constrain such policies. Firstly, there is often a strong demand for drugs, irrespective of health considerations. Secondly, drug production and distribution are massively profitable endeavours which have the support of both legal and illegal vested interests. Legal drug production is profitable not only to the manufacturers and distributors. Governments, local authorities and numerous allied industries derive considerable revenue from contracts, taxes and other benefits (Bruun et al. 1975). In some areas the production of drugs, be they alcohol, tobacco, cocaine, cannabis, opium or tranquillisers, provides crucial employment in areas where otherwise there may be few if any alternatives. When a drug is widely used and is legal, health may not be a very powerful political consideration. Even when a drug, such as heroin, is illegal, it is difficult to control supply, because this is organised covertly, and may also be supported by massive vested interests associated with a high risk but also high profit industry (Adler 1985, Freemantle 1985). Attempts to reduce the availability of alcohol and tobacco have faced strong opposition from the respective trades and from a wide range of political interests

167

(Taylor 1984, Raistrick and Davidson 1985). Very often the value of a legal drug to the national economy appears to far outweigh the cost of misuse even if the latter is enormous and largely intangible (Grant, Plant and Williams 1982, Royal College of Psychiatrists 1986). The difficulty and ultimate futility of attempting to proscribe the use of a highly popular drug has been graphically exemplified by the American experience of Prohibition. This was good for liver cirrhosis (which declined) but had little chance of survival for political and economic reasons. Rationing or putting up the price of a highly popular drug is not usually politically attractive. The type of restraints which have been imposed vary markedly and reflect national traditions and attitudes. In addition, draconian controls lead to the establishment of black markets and to an upsurge of criminal activity.

There are many problems related to attempts to restrict the availability of psychoactive drugs. This should not distract attention from the crucial point that drug *use* is associated with levels of drug *misuse*. The latter will almost inevitably be high if the former is high. Some gains may be made by enforcing laws to curb specific forms of drug-related behaviour. Sadly, these appear to be fairly marginal compared with those attainable by keeping the overall level of drug use to an acceptable level in terms of the inevitable toll of problems. The latter may only be restricted by constraints upon personal freedom, by law enforcement, customs searches, expense and inconvenience (Bakalar and Grinspoon 1984).

In some countries there are very few services available to provide help for those with drug-related problems. Such agencies are largely concentrated in developed countries or in those in which specific drug problems have long been a major cause of public and political concern. Services for drug-related problems have to compete with the demands of a profusion of other health and social problems. Drug users are often not perceived as a high priority or deserving group. Many clinicians do not feel confident about working with problem drug users and for various reasons such individuals are not regarded as popular patients or clients.

In most countries there is little education about drugs for those in the helping professions. In addition, there is little evidence in many countries related to patterns of drug use and misuse or to the effectiveness of a wider range of relevant policy options. The uncertain efficacy of not only treatment agencies but also of other forms of response, such as law enforcement, frequently makes it difficult to justify the expenditure in a field in which gains are so unclear. In addition, there are sometimes counterproductive rivalries between people in different disciplines and with different philosophies, which make it difficult to assess the respective merits of alternative strategies to the provision of help for drug problems. Drug policy is now further confused by the emergence of AIDS. This has enhanced the importance of devising strategies to curb high-risk forms of drug use, but has intensified the moral dilemmas surrounding the implementation of policy (Advisory Council on the Misuse of Drugs 1988, Plant 1990).

This chapter has, by design, largely emphasised factors which inhibit policy formulation and implementation. It is emphasised that a number of major areas of policy exist which can and should benefit from research. As noted above, research frequently does not exert a major influence on policy. In fact, virtually all policy options and public expenditure on 'drug problems' could benefit considerably from research. In particular, major policy options should, if possible, be evaluated, and the results of past evaluations should be used to design future policy. No country has unlimited resources to devote to AIDS, alcohol, tobacco, prescribed and illicit drug misuse. Accordingly, research has a major contribution to make by measuring and describing drug problems and in devising practical strategies to minimise such problems.

## Conclusion

Policies to regulate the use and misuse of drugs may be implemented at local, regional, national and international levels. A daunting number of difficulties hinder the implementation of such policies. These are largely in the form of competing demands for resources and factors which oppose interests of public health. Ultimately, as noted by Bruun *et al.* (1975) and Kendell (1979), the solutions to alcohol problems are political rather than medical. This is equally true in relation to tobacco, prescribed and illegal drugs. Perhaps the greatest improvement in policy formulation in most countries would be the adoption of a co-ordinated approach to drug policy. As noted above, drug use and misuse are multifaceted and impinge upon a wide range of local, national and international agencies. At present, drug policy is too often dealt with by segregating the substances (alcohol, tobacco, prescribed and illicit drugs) or by agencies in isolation from others. Few countries could fairly claim yet to have adopted a properly co-ordinated approach to all forms of drug misuse.

REFERENCES

Adler, P. (1985) *Wheeling and Dealing: An Ethnography of an Upper-Level Drug Dealing and Smuggling Community*, New York: Columbia University Press.

Advisory Council on the Misuse of Drugs (1988) *AIDS and Drug Misuse Part 1*, London: HMSO.

Bakalar, J. and Grinspoon, L. (1984) *Drug Control in a Free Society*, Cambridge: Cambridge University Press.

Bandy, P. and President, P.A. (1983) Recent literature on drug abuse prevention and mass media: focussing on youth, parents, women and the elderly, *Journal of Drug Education* 13, 255–71.

Brain, P.F. (ed) (1986) *Alcohol and Aggression*, London: Croom Helm.

Bruun, K., Edwards, G., Lumio, M., Mäkelä, K., Pan, L., Popham, R.E., Room, R., Schmidt, W., Skog, O-J., Sulkenen, P. and Österberg, E. (1975) *Alcohol Control Policies in a Public Health Perspective*, Helsinki: Finnish Foundation for Alcohol Studies.

Bruun, K., Pan, L. and Rexed, I. (1975) *The Gentleman's Club: International Control of Drugs and Alcohol*, Chicago: University of Chicago Press.

Cahalan, D. and Room, R. (1974) *Problem Drinking Among American Men*, Monograph No. 7, New Brunswick, New Jersey: Rutgers Centre for Alcohol Studies.

Collins, J.J. (Jun.)(ed)(1981) *Drinking and Crime*, London: Tavistock.

Davies, J.B. and Stacey, B. (1972) *Teenagers and Alcohol: A Developmental Study in Glasgow*, London: HMSO.

Fazey, C. (1977) *The Aetiology of Psychoactive Substance Use*, Paris: UNESCO.

Freemantle, B. (1985) *The Fix*, London: Michael Joseph.

Gillies, P.A. and Willcox, B. (1984) Reducing the risk of smoking amongst the young, *Public Health* 98, 49–54.

Glaser, D. and Snow, M. (1969) *Public Knowledge and Attitudes on Drug Abuse*, New York: New York State Addiction Control Commission.

Goode, E. (1972) *Drugs in American Society*, New York: Alfred A. Knopf.

Gossop, M. (1987) *Living with Drugs*, London: Temple Smith.

Grant, M., Plant, M.A. and Williams, A. (eds) (1982) *Economics and Alcohol*, London: Croom Helm.

Hore, B.D. and Plant, M.A. (eds) (1980) *Alcohol Problems in Employment*, London: Croom Helm.Kalb, M. (1975) The myth of alcoholism prevention, *Preventative Medicine*, 4, 404–16.

Kandel, D.B. (1982) Epidemiological and psychosocial perspectives on adolescent drug use, *Journal of the American Academy of Child Psychiatry* 21, 328–47.

Kendell, R.E. (1979) Alcoholism: a medical or a political problem?, *British Medical Journal*, 367–71.

Kessel, N. and Walton, H. (1965) *Alcoholism*, Harmondsworth, Middx.: Pelican.

Kinder, B.N., Pape, N.E. and Walfish, S. (1980) Drug and alcohol education programmes: a review of outcome studies, *International Journal of the Addictions*, 15, 1035–54.

Levine, S. and Lilienfield, A. (eds) (1987) *Epidemiology and Health Policy*, London: Tavistock.

Peck, D.F. (1982) Some determining factors. In Plant, M.A. (ed) *Drinking and Problem Drinking*, pp. 65–83, London: Junction/Fourth Estate.

Plant, M.A. (1981) What aetiologies? In Edwards, G. and Busch, C. (eds) *Drug Problems in Britain: A Review of Ten Years*, pp. 245–80, London: Academic Press.

170

Plant, M.A. (ed) (1982) *Drinking and Problem Drinking*, London: Junction/Fourth Estate.

Plant, M.A. (1987) *Drugs in Perspective*, London: Hodder and Stoughton.

Plant, M.A. (ed.) (1990) *AIDS, Drugs and Prostitution*, London: Routledge.

Raistrick, D. and Davidson, R. (1985) *Alcoholism and Drug Addiction*, Edinburgh: Churchill Livingstone.

Ross, H.L. (1984) *Deterring the Drunken Driver*, Lexington, Mass.: Lexington Books.

Royal College of Psychiatrists (1986) *Alcohol: Our Favourite Drug*, London: Tavistock.

Royal College of Physicians (1983) *Health or Smoking?*, London: Pitman Medical.

Schaps, E., Dibartolo, R., Moskowitz, J., Balley, C.G. and Churgin, G. (1981) A review of 127 drug abuse prevention programme evaluations, *Journal of Drug Issues* 11, 17–43.

Smart, R.G. (1979) Priorities for minimising alcohol problems among young people. In Blane, H.T. and Chafetz, M.E. (eds) *Youth, Alcohol and Public Policy*, New York: Plenum.

Smith, R. (1987) *Unemployment and Health*, Oxford: Oxford University Press.

Swisher, J.D. (1971) Drug education: pushing or preventing?, *Peabody Journal of Education* 68–75.

Taylor, P. (1984) *Smoke Ring: The Policies of Tobacco*, London: Bodley Head.

Thomspon, E.L. (1978) Smoking education programmes 1960–1976, *American Journal of Public Health* 68, 250–1.

Vaillant, G. (1970) The natural history of narcotic drug addiction, *Seminars in Psychiatry* 2, 486–98.

Weil, A. (1972) *The Natural Mind*, Harmondsworth, Middx.: Penguin.

Young, J. (1971) *The Drugtakers*, London: Paladin.

171

# 16. Conclusion

MARTIN PLANT

The contributors to this book have reviewed a wide range of issues related to the conduct and implications of research into the use and misuse of alcohol, tobacco, prescribed and illegal drugs. While the individual contributions have been presented in relation to authors' national settings, a number of themes have been highlighted as fairly general concerns. In addition, a consensus of views is evident in relation to a number of practical issues which relate to the conduct of future epidemiological studies.

Firstly, it is clear that, in most European countries, both surveys and other research methods have been far more widely applied to alcohol than to other psychoactive drugs, including tobacco. This is not surprising, since alcohol is the most widely used drug and its use is associated with a variety of related problems. Because of the pre-eminence of alcohol much of the text of this book has emphasised this rather than other drugs. Even so, as several contributors have asserted, experience in alcohol research has major and obvious implications for research related to other drugs.

Several basic research problems have been highlighted which require far more attention in the future than they have received in the past. Foremost amongst these are the issues of the validity (truthfulness) and reliability (consistency) of the data obtained by surveys or other methods. Respondents to studies of self-reported psychoactive substance use often under-report and over-report. This greatly flaws the type of information obtained by researchers. In addition it is reasonable to suppose that such biases may be especially great in relation to 'deviant' or illegal behaviour, such as heavy, problematic or illegal forms of drug use. Surveys are established as invaluable tools of epidemiology. Even so, far

172

more needs to be done to assess and to improve the adequacy of different approaches. As John Duffy has noted, there are indications that novel approaches may elicit fuller information than is produced by conventional face-to-face interviews. The use of computer interviewing (CSAQ) and randomized response (RR) should be investigated further, and other strategies should also be evaluated. Many surveys in North America are now conducted, not face-to-face, but by telephone interviews. This approach may be less justifiable in countries in which many people do not have access to telephones. Even so, this potentially useful strategy could be used experimentally in Europe. As noted by Hildigunnur Ólafsdóttir, it has already been employed in Iceland. There is also some British evidence indicating that such surveys are methodologically as well as financially worthwhile (Market Research Development Fund 1985).

Even within a single country survey research is beset by problems of bias, non-compliance and failure to locate potentially interesting respondents. These problems become compounded when investigations seek to collect information from heterogenous populations, either within a single country, such as the USSR, or within several countries, such as those included in the Scandanavian Drinking Survey or the study of the Community Response to Alcohol-Related Problems (Ritson 1985).

As emphasized by Anokhina, Ivanets, Keup and other contributors 'good data' need to be based upon clear and unequivocal definitions. The latter then have to be applied uniformly if statistical information is to be really meaningful. In practice, individual indicators of legal and illegal drug use and misuse are invariably deeply flawed by variations of interpretation and implementation. A study by Latcham, Kreitman, Plant and Crawford (1984) has indicated that, in Britain, regional variations in psychiatric hospital rates for alcohol dependence were largely artefacts of local differences in hospital admission policy. Davies and Walsh (1983) have drawn attention to similar problems which beset attempts to compare measures of 'alcohol problems' in different countries.

In some respects survey methodology may still be regarded as 'experimental'. Perhaps this is an overstatement, but it is clear from the preceding chapters that there is considerable scope for the improvement of research methods. In many countries it is difficult enough for researchers to obtain funds to mount a 'descriptive' survey. Regrettably, it is often far harder to secure support for research projects aimed primarily at improving methods. This situation needs to be rectified, and perhaps the World Health Organization could help to bring about a change in this situation by actively encouraging research into methodology.

Researchers, like other people, are individualistic. Few are content simply to copy the work of others, and most, for good reasons, are inclined to at least adopt the procedures used by their predecessors. Accordingly, it is probably unrealistic to expect that rigorous uniformity in survey or other methods will ever be attained. It is probable that future studies will continue to exhibit considerable variation of approach. In spite of this, comparative studies, either geographical or temporal ones, require a 'core' of standardized definitions and recording procedures. There are already some excellent contributors in this field (e.g. Hughes, Venulet, Khan, Medina-Mora, Navaratnam, Poshyachinda, Rootman, Salan and Wadud 1980).

The World Health Organization would be the ideal agency whereby the formulation of such a basic set of procedures for use in alcohol surveys could be constructed. These could probably be in the form of a manual which provides a wide-ranging set of questions on alcohol use and misuse and upon other relevant variables such as the biographical traits of survey respondents. Such a manual would be constructed on the basis of past work, so that data collected in accordance with the guidelines would be comparable with at least some available evidence. If such a manual was produced its use should be fostered both by individual researchers and by the encouragement of the World Health Organization. Similar manuals could usefully be produced to facilitate survey research in relation to tobacco, prescribed and illegal drugs.

As emphasised by several of the contributors to this book, there has been far more epidemiological research in Europe into the use and misuse of alcohol than into that of other psychoactive substances. In consequence, research into other such drugs, especially illegal ones, remains relatively undeveloped. This presents a striking contrast with North America, where surveys of drug use are well established and a rich literature has been generated. A considerable body of European drug research has been conducted (e.g. Edwards and Busch 1981). Even so, in the United States surveys are routinely used to collect both comparable cross-sectional and longitudinal data on patterns of self-reported drug use (Kandel 1978, Miller, Cisin, Gardner Keaton, Harrell, Wirtz, Abelsen and Fishburne 1983, Johnson, O'Malley and Bachman 1984). European studies should, in future, be less myopically focused upon alcohol. More emphasis is already warranted upon illegal drugs. In addition, far more future studies should encompass alcohol together with tobacco, prescribed and illegal drug use, since, as noted by Wolfram Keup and others (Kandell 1978, Plant 1987) one type of psychoactive drug use is often, and perhaps increasingly, linked to other forms – apart from the fact that at an individual level, several forms of drug use may be combined. It is also possible that the levels of *per capita* alcohol, tobacco, prescribed and illegal drug use might also be linked due to a substitutional relationship. This possibility warrants investigation and has major implications in relation to the possible side-effects of alcohol and tobacco control policies. There is a clear link between psychoactive drug use and the risks of HIV infection and AIDS (e.g. Robertson 1987, Robertson and Plant 1988, Siegal 1988, Plant 1990). Far more work is needed to clarify these risks and to devise effective harm minimisation and prevention strategies.

Surveys and other epidemiological approaches have an invaluable role to play in monitoring the patterns and trends of psychoactive drug use and misuse. In theory, effective policies require an underpinning of full and accurate information. Sadly, many of the policies and initiatives in the drug and alcohol fields are not greatly influenced by epidemiology or by any research. As noted by Kendell (1979) and Taylor (1984) policies on alcohol and tobacco are influenced by a host of factors apart from health, and, ultimately, social policy is frequently determined by political considerations. An excellent collection of reviews edited by Levine and Lilienfield (1987) has discussed the relationship between *Epidemiology and Health Policy*. The editors reached this sombre conclusion (pp. 3–5):

> Epidemiologists are mindful of the methodological constraints to their developing a more powerful discipline. Indeed few fields are as conscientious in their attention to questioning and improving methods of data collection and analysis. The self-critical stance which pervades the discipline is even evident in the frequent efforts to define and delineate the special domain of epidemiology. But if we are to understand the failure of epidemiology to achieve its potential in influencing health policy, we must go beyond epide-

miological or technological constraints of the discipline, in search of explanations with political and social foundations. . . One such explanation may lie in the professional standing of the field. Ironically, despite its potential to serve as a guide to improve the health of society, epidemiology by a number of indicators has enjoyed relatively low status as compared with clinical medicine as well as with other branches of clinical science. . . Also epidemiological recommendations often require relinquishing some gratifying experience like smoking, drinking alcohol, or satisfying the palate, with the promise that in the distant future some health benefits may possibly be achieved. With regard to these recommendations, epidemiological prescriptions not only have to contend with the habits and gratifications of individual consumers but equally if not more importantly with the resistance and opposition by powerful commercial interest such as tobacco and alcoholic beverage manufacturers and distributors.

This is a depressing yet realistic view. Research by itself is conducted in a vacuum. Those who engage in research into the use and misuse of alcohol and other psychoactive drugs work in a socially sensitive and highly politicized arena. Such researchers face two challenges. The first of these is to improve their methods, and the second is to communicate their results more cogently.

As indicated in the previous chapter, drug policy formulation in most countries is ill co-ordinated. The different substances (alcohol, tobacco, prescribed and illegal drugs) are often regarded as quite separate from a policy perspective. In addition, many of the agencies which are involved with different aspects of drug policy fail to co-ordinate their strategies. Accordingly, finance ministries, health and social service ministries not uncommonly prepare drug policies which are conflicting. Recent examples include the provision of public funds in Britain to build a factory to produce a form of tobacco product which was banned only a few months later, and a proposal to 'harmonize' alcohol taxation within the European Community. Research is more likely to influence future drug policy development if the latter becomes co-ordinated at a local, national and international level.

Finally, drug policy should in future always be devised with full reference to available research evidence. This should be an absolute imperative for policy makers and is a challenge for researchers.

REFERENCES

Davies, P.T. and Walsh, D. (1983) *Alcohol Problems and Alcohol Control Policies in Europe*, London: Croom Helm.

Edwards, G. and Busch, C. (eds)(1981) *Drug Problems in Britian*, London: Academic Press.

Hughes, P.H., Venulet, J., Khan, V., Medina-Mora, M.E., Navaratnam, V., Poshyachinda, V., Rootman, I., Salan, R. and Wadud, K.A. (1980) *Core Data for Epidemiological Studies of Non-Medical Drug Use*, WHO Offset Publication No. 56, Geneva: WHO.

Johnson, L.D., O'Malley, P.M. and Bachman, J.G. (1984) *Drugs and American High School Students 1975–1985*, National Institute on Drug Abuse, US Department of Health and Human Services, Public Health Service, Alcohol, Drug and Mental Health Administration.

Kandell, D.B. (ed) (1978) *Longitudinal Drug Research*, New York: Halstead.

Kendell, R.E. (1979) Alcoholism: A medical or a political problem? *British Medical Journal* 279, 367–371.

Latcham, R., Kreitman, N., Plant, M.A. and Crawford, A. (1984) Regional variations in alcohol-related morbidity in Britain: A myth uncovered? I. Clinical surveys, *British Medical Journal* 289, 1341–3.

Levine, S. and Lilienfield, A. (eds) (1987) *Epidemiology and Health Policy*, London: Tavistock.

Market Research Development Fund (1985) *Comparing Telephone and Face to Face Interviews*, London: Market Research Development Fund.

Miller, J.D., Cisin, I.H., Gardner Keaton, H., Harrell, A.V., Wirtz, P.W., Abelsen, H.I. and Fishburne, H.I. (1983) *US National Survey on Drug Abuse: Main Findings*. National Institute on Drug Abuse, Department of Health and Human Services, Alcohol, Drug and Mental Health Administration.

Plant, M.A. (1987) *Drugs in Perspective*, London: Hodder and Stoughton.

Plant, M.A. (ed) (1990) *AIDS, Drugs and Prostitution*, London: Routledge.

Ritson, E.B. (1985) *Community Responses to Alcohol-Related Problems: Review of an International Study*, Public Health Papers 81, Geneva: WHO.

Robertson, J.A. and Plant, M.A. (1988) Alcohol, sex and risks of HIV infection, *Drug and Alcohol Dependence* 22, 75–8.

Robertson, J.R. (1987) *Heroin, AIDS and Society*, London: Hodder and Stoughton.

Siegal, L. (ed) (1988) *AIDS and Substance Abuse*, New York: Harrington Park Press.

Taylor, D. (1984) *Smoke Ring: The Politics of Tobacco*, London: Bodley Head.

177

# APPENDIX

Participants and contributors to WHO Consultation on Problems Related to Alcohol and Psychoactive Drugs, Edinburgh, 27–30 May 1986

Professor Irina Anokhina, All-Union Research Centre on Narcology, Kropotkinsky per 23, 119034 Moscow, USSR

Dr Marie Choquet, Institut National de la Santé et de la Recherche Médicale (INSERM), Villejuif Cedex, Paris, France

Mr John Duffy, Medical Research Council Unit for Epidemiological Studies in Psychiatry, Department of Psychiatry, The Kennedy Tower, University of Edinburgh, Morningside Park, Edinburgh EH10 5HF, Scotland, United Kingdom

Dr Nikolai Ivanets, All-Union Research Centre on Narcology, Kropotkinsky per 23, 119034 Moscow, USSR

Professor Wolfram Keup, Feldafinger Str. 25a, D-8134 Pocking/Starnberg, Federal Republic of Germany

Ms Hildigunnur Ólafsdóttir, Landspitalinn, National University Hospital, Department of Psychiatry, 101 Reykjavik, Iceland

Dr Esa Österberg, Social Research Institute of Alcohol Studies, Kalevankatu 12, SF-00100 Helsinki, Finland

Dr Martin Plant (Local Organizer), Alcohol Research Group, Department of Psychiatry, University of Edinburgh, Morningside Park, Edinburgh, EH10 5HF, Scotland, UK

Dr Walter Weiss, Swiss Institute for Public Health and Hospitals, P.O. Box 1063, 1001 Lausanne, Switzerland

*Author of discussion paper*

Dr Nick Dorn, Institute for the Study of Drug Dependence, 1–4 Hatton Place, Hatton Garden, London, EC1N 8ND, UK

*Observers*

Dr Roy Melville and Dr Elizabeth Sowler, Scottish Home and Health Department, St Andrew's House, Edinburgh, EH1 3DE, Scotland, UK

Dr Pamela Green, Department of Social Security, (DSS), Alexander Fleming House, Elephant and Castle, London SE1 6BY, UK

Dr Robert Power, (on behalf of the DSS), Drug Indicators Project, Birkbeck College, 16 Gower Street, London LC1, UK

*Representatives of other organisations*

*WHO Collaborating Centre for Research and Training in Mental Health, Mannheim*

Dr. Hans Veiel, Central Institute of Mental Health, J5 – P.O. Box 5970, D-6800 Mannheim, Federal Republic of Germany

*International Council on Alcohol and the Addictions*

Mr. Peter Rørstad, North East Council on Addictions, 1 Mosley Street, Newcastle upon Tyne NE1 1YE, UK

*World Health Organization*

*Regional Office for Europe*

Mr. Cees Goos, Scientist, Abuse of Psychoactive Drugs, Mental Health Unit, World Health Organization, 8, Scherfigsvej, DK-2100 Copenhagen O, Denmark

Mrs. Ann Holst, Secretary, Abuse of Psychoactive Drugs, Mental Health Unit, World Health Organization, 8, Scherfigsvej, DK-2100 Copenhagen O, Denmark

*Secretaries to Alcohol Research Group*

Mrs. Valerie Mannings
Mrs. Janis Nichol

# INDEX

*Note*: Page references in *italics* indicate tables and figures.